D1566330

WINDMILLS, DROUTHS AND COTTONSEED CAKE

WINDMILLS, DROUTHS AND COTTONSEED CAKE

A Biased Biography of a
West Texas Rancher

by

JOHN A. HALEY

Foreword by B. Byron Price
Illustrations by Duane Bryers

Texas Christian University Press
Fort Worth, Texas

Library of Congress Cataloging-in-Publication Data

Haley, John A.
    Windmills, drouths, and cottenseed cake ; a biased
biography of a West Texas rancher / by John A. Haley.
        p. cm.
    ISBN 0-87565-141-0
    1. Haley, John Furman, 1897-1972. 2. Ranch life— Texas.
3. Ranchers —Texas—Biography. 4. Texas, West—Biography.
I. Title.
F391.4.H35H35 1995
976.4'06'092— dc20
[B]   94-30504
                                                                    CIP

Designed by Shadetree Studio
Fort Worth, Texas

This book is dedicated to every cowboy
who, during the heat of summer,
washed his saddleblankets
more often than he
washed his socks.

Foreword

My maternal grandfather, Dewey Seay, the namesake of an admiral in the Spanish-American War but better known to his grandkids as "Pappy," was a stock-farmer in the Texas Panhandle. As children we idolized him and, on summer visits to the country in the 1950s, eagerly followed his lead through irrigated fields of wheat and corn. Amid the shady stalks that often towered above us, we avoided snakes and snares by following closely in Pappy's footsteps. The strategy never failed.

Along the way we often picked up cockleburs, grasshoppers and bits of wisdom about animals and weather. When pressed, Pappy was a wonderful storyteller who delighted in recounting tales of bygone days when mule teams plowed the fields and automobiles were a rarity on the high plains. His most vivid anecdotes still cling in my memory, like the tenacious cockleburs that once snared the cuffs of my Levis.

Some of his curious customs, like drinking coffee from a saucer after pouring it from a cup and blowing it cool, tickle me yet. The beauty and bounty of his flower and vegetable garden live on as well, not only in my recollection but also in my mother's green thumb.

Pappy taught me much more about work and faith, optimism and endurance than he did about farming. When life grows difficult or complex, I often take refuge in his wisdom. Although the perspectives of age and experience have made me aware of some of his flaws and his lifestyle does not seem quite as romantic as it did when I was younger, I still admire him. Increasingly, I also feel the need to share his story and something of his character with the next generation of our family. His traditions are worth passing on.

A similar impulse guided John Haley in writing this biography of his father. And yet the author's effort transcends mere genealogy to illuminate universal themes and emotions, played out against a backdrop of momentous change.

The further time and space take us from our rural roots and a day-to-day relationship with nature, the less we seem to comprehend the challenges and motivations of the country life that produced my grandfather and John Furman Haley. They were both products of the nineteenth century, born into a world far different from our own. Their lives and personalities were shaped not only by their southern roots, Victorian family values and Jeffersonian political traditions, but also by the incessant demands of wresting a living from the often hostile semi-arid plains of West Texas.

Tough and enduring, much like the land itself, the farmers and ranchers of West Texas who withstood the rigors of the Great Depression, two world wars and countless droughts, subscribed to a code of conduct that mixed rugged individualism with neighborly cooperation. Although shy of formal education, most possessed a natural ability to manage livestock, machinery and men. Conservative in philosophy, politics and habit, they also manifested an Old Testament view of right and wrong, though work was their true religion.

If spare with words and feelings, they nevertheless were open and friendly to strangers. Their humor was as dry as their range and, given the tenuous nature of their chosen profession and the scarcity of rain, they maintained a seemingly unnatural optimism about the future. This bent led them to close many a trade with only a handshake. After all, "you can't contract with a son-of-a-bitch," as my father once put it.

Few of the modern travelers hustling across the parched emptiness of the Permian Basin on a thin ribbon of concrete and asphalt ever encounter more than a glimpse of its scattered rural inhabitants. Even then, the speed and course of these intruders blur and limit their view. Genuine insight into the life and customs of the region demands a slower, more rhythmic pace, like the long loping gait of a gentle saddle horse or the measured stroke of an oil-field pump jack.

From cattle range to oil patch, John Haley's lean narrative is replete with such rhythm and insight. In an era of sensational, tell-all biographies remarkable only for their utter superficiality, Haley writes of his dad with sympathy, understanding and respect. But if his narrative possesses none of the rancor and self-deluding fantasy that characterizes today's typical family exposé, there are honesty and truth in abundance, even when the subject is unpleasant or controversial.

With the traditions of his clan and the code by which he lived as a snubbing post, John Furman Haley stepped aboard life as he would a rank bronco. Neither saint nor hero, he always gave an honest try and, even when thrown hard, never quit. What he lacked in style he made up for with stamina, courage and principle. Unsung in life, his legacy lives on in this humble memoir, a fitting reminder of uncommon character and a life well-lived.

B. Byron Price
The National Cowboy Hall of Fame
Oklahoma City, Oklahoma
October 1994

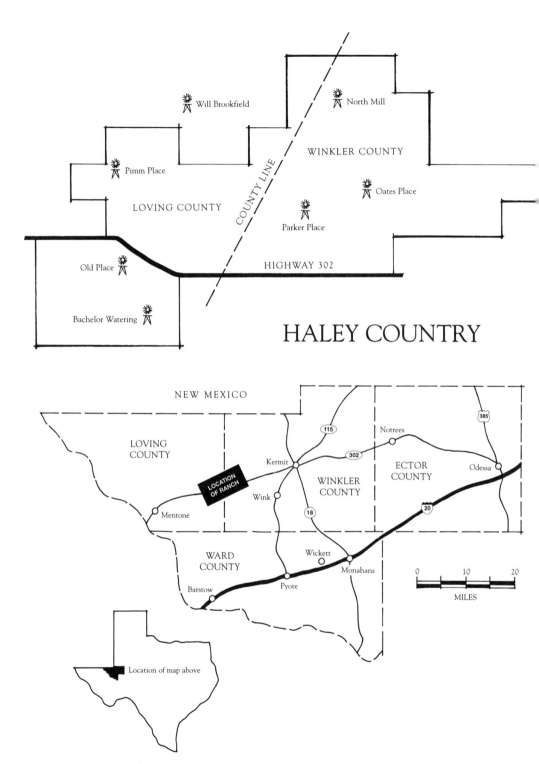

Will Brookfield

North Mill

COUNTY LINE

WINKLER COUNTY

Pimm Place

LOVING COUNTY

Oates Place

Parker Place

HIGHWAY 302

Old Place

Bachelor Watering

HALEY COUNTRY

NEW MEXICO

LOVING
COUNTY

115

Notrees

385

302

Kermit

ECTOR
COUNTY

Odessa

LOCATION
OF RANCH

WINKLER
COUNTY

Wink

Mentone

18

20

WARD
COUNTY

Wickett

Monahans

Barstow

Pyote

0   10   20

MILES

Location of map above

Preface

John Furman Haley lived from 1897 to 1972. That was surely the most exciting, the most intriguing seventy-five-year time span in recorded history. The electric light bulb, steam engine, telegraph, telephone, repeating rifle and cotton gin each has its well-deserved and appointed place in the progress of man, but twentieth century technology eclipsed them all. It transformed the world, and John lived from wagon roads to superhighways, from chugging locomotives to rocket-powered journeys into outer space.

Unfortunately, there has been a corresponding decline in the attitudes and ethics of American citizens, and a demoralizing bureaucracy has taken full advantage. My comments in the following pages about some of the stultifying results of this moral decay are few, and though they are heartfelt, the purpose is to illustrate the gradual change in priorities and customs. We are, of course, talking about trends and majorities. There are still many people in the United States who would ecstatically exchange every government guarantee for the return of their independence.

John Haley was such a man, and his attitude epitomized the creed of western ranchers and cowboys of his time. What tended to set him apart was his extraordinary self-reliance, endless energy, and willingness—even eagerness—to meet any challenge life held in store. He moved no mountains, toppled no governments nor built any empires; yet he was an embodiment of the character and spirit that creates the distinctive aura which identifies those proud individuals who value freedom above all else. These were the characteristics John's friends and family admired and enjoyed.

It is possible that in years to come historians might find a few items of interest herein, though there is nothing of historical significance. Neither has there been any attempt to portray ranch life per se, nor to cover every phase of John's active life. My goal was to write a more or less chronological account of his peregrinations, avoid repetition and tedium, call attention to the changing times, and above all, to present a clear image of the man himself. It is my anxious hope that end has been accomplished.

As my fingers prowl aimlessly through the manuscript, my eyes are drawn to this passage or the other, and I am filled with a sense of inadequacy. Something seems to be missing. Was Daddy shortchanged in this abbreviated biography? Is the presentation articulate? How could I miss every loop at several good stories? Those and other nagging questions produce the same helpless sensation as the snap of a curb strap on a cold-jawed horse.

Disturbing thoughts—and they offer the suggestion that my remarks about ranch hands without proper credentials were a little too harsh. Ah well, there is no getting around it—I am fair game for any of those would-be cowboys who might have hit the big time in a literary field.

I must confess that others provided the will and technical skill to see this story in print. Shortly after Daddy's death my uncle, J. Evetts Haley, announced: "John, a story should be done on your dad." I was overjoyed; nobody does a cowboy biography better than J. Evetts. Then he added, "And you are the one who should do it." I was disappointed, to say the least, but the seed was sown and much to my surprise, it sprouted. Research began immediately and within two months the first draft of the first chapter was scattered across the kitchen table. Approximately forty rewrites later the first chapter was still on the kitchen table, a jumbled mess, mutilated by gnashing teeth and tears of frustration. For some unfathomable reason, the thing had not grown and flourished. "Lack of nutrition," some of my kith and kin diagnosed, "due to mental drouths and barren soil." Maybe so, but I personally believe there was something wrong with that confounded table. It was time for a break.

My uncle did not neglect the problem. He poked and prodded, furnished material and offered timely suggestions. I was still on a break. Evetts almost despaired, but the near surrender was premature. My wife liked his idea from the outset, and Stefanie is a formidable force. Besides, she reduced the situation to an ancient domestic conundrum. How long can a procrastinating pessimist parry the persistence of his peremptory spouse? Quite a while it seems, but the outcome was never in serious doubt. Twenty-odd years later, the seed Evetts planted and Stefanie nourished finally bore fruit.

It is self-evident that only the author is accountable for factual errors, but I bow to tradition and hereby tender my culpability. However, should punctuation and grammar earn recognition, the responsibility lies elsewhere. Any fallout from that pleasant surprise must descend on the capable shoulders of Beth Schneider. She is my editor, critic and adviser, a marvel with syntax who rarely permits grammatical transgressions. Beth is also a much loved and highly valued friend who has done a yeoman's job preparing this book for print.

Without the interest and efforts of these sterling supporters, much of John's trail would have disappeared under tomorrow's shifting sands.

J.A.H.
Kermit, Texas

Power is, in nature, the essential measure of right.
Nature suffers nothing to remain in her kingdoms
which cannot help itself.

—Ralph Waldo Emerson

I feare no foe, I fawne no friend;
I lothe not life, nor dread mine end.

—Sir Edward Dyer

I

"Damn, I wish it would rain!" Since 1866, when Charles Goodnight and Oliver Loving pushed their first trail herd up the bitter waters of the Pecos en route to Fort Sumner, this cowboy plea for moisture has been uttered countless thousands of times. The need for more rain in West Texas probably arose six months after Noah reportedly ran his boat aground on Ararat and has existed ever since. This particular lament came from my father, John Haley, Jr.

We were walking around what is now known as the Bachelor watering, located in southeastern Loving County approximately twenty miles southwest of Kermit and twenty miles northwest of Pyote. This is also the site of the ten-by-fourteen shack which was Daddy's first home on the ranch that my grandfather, J.A. Haley, traded for in 1915. They stocked the place the following year and Daddy moved into the shack; to my delight on this torrid day in 1969 he was fondly reliving old memories.

"The shack stood just about here and faced south," Daddy explained, indicating a spot about 100 feet southeast of the tank. Nothing remained but a few burnt rocks and bits of broken glass turned purple by years of exposure to the sun. As he stood there lost in thought, he shoved his hat back and rubbed his head in a familiar but inimitable way, and a broad grin lit up his weathered face.

"I remember one time when I drove in from Pyote with the groceries and noticed that somebody had come by and eaten dinner while I was gone. Well, back then it was customary to eat at anybody's camp you rode up on. If someone was there he would invite you to get down and eat, and if there wasn't anyone there you were welcome to fix your own meal. The trouble was that whoever ate dinner at my camp that day left the dishes and frying pan dirty. Well, by God, you just didn't do that! If you ate, then you damned sure cleaned up the mess.

"So I saddled ol' Hammer, got my six-shooter and struck a lope west follerin' his horse tracks across the sand. I knew if I could catch him before sundown that gentleman was going to come back and clean up my camp.

"Well, I had follered him about three or four miles and was trottin' along thinkin', lettin' ol' Hammer have a breather, when I figured out who it was. It was L.W. Anderson." (Mr. Anderson was a neighbor and former employer, a man Daddy always liked and greatly admired.) "I had been studyin' about it all along and just couldn't think who would do such a thing until I thought of him, and I knew he'd done it as a prank. Even after I figured out who it was, it didn't help my feelin's much for awhile. Then I got to thinkin' about L.W. trottin' in to the Dixie ranch, across the river, chucklin' all the way, knowin' I'd be mad and follerin' him. So I just pulled ol' Hammer up and went back.

"I don't remember whether I ever mentioned it to him or not. I don't think so. I figured if he never knew how mad I'd

2

got it wouldn't be as funny to him." Daddy stood there for a few seconds looking off into the glaring heat. "Well, we'd better be gettin' back, I guess. Damn we need a rain!"

That was characteristic. He always enjoyed spinning yarns about the past or present, but he never had time for idle reflection. There was always something to be done right then.

He was at this time past seventy and probably had little or nothing to do when he got "back." Nevertheless, he was impatient to get to it.

The country itself is not conducive to patience. Semi-desert in aspect, it is a study of extremes. Seasons here are not clearly defined. The fall of the year is the most pleasant and consistent, but even then the nights are often very cold and the days uncomfortably warm. Fall somehow merges into winter unnoticed, and it isn't at all unusual to drive into town in the morning with the heater and defroster going full blast and return to the ranch that afternoon with the air conditioner on. The coldest spells in January sometimes dip below zero, while the seductive warmth of February is apt to lure the tender leaves from the elms in time to face the biting frosts of March. Spring is usually a series of sandstorms that separate February from May, with enough late northers thrown in to remind you that all the extra coats, scarves, gloves and caps in your pickup are not useless clutter. It has even been known to rain, but only the most incurable optimists go prepared for such an unlikely event. When strangers inquire about the average annual rainfall, we grin sheepishly and admit that we don't know. This simply isn't a land of averages.

Beneath these more or less predictable clear-to-dusty skies lie gently rolling hills covered with undernourished mesquite, catclaw and greasewood. The light covering of grama grass turf is either dirty gray or a bright healthy green. The cattle and horses, and for that matter even the coyotes and rodents that range here, will more than likely be rolling fat or dangerously thin. With such barren land and perverse weather, people wonder why anyone would want to ranch in this country. Yet they do, and most of them stay.

When a person's living comes from the soil, as my own family's and many others' did, there is a considerable strain on endurance. Not just physical—there are other areas in America where physical endurance is more severely taxed—but mental wear and tear. "God! Will it rain in time?" This isn't a cry that is heard once in a decade. It is heard every two or three years. And yet they stay. Despite the merciless heat, the searing winds, and sometimes bitter cold, they stay.

Why? Agricultural opportunities are severely limited, and the country's most ardent lovers are rarely victimized by aesthetic rapture. What is the bewitching fascination of an unforgiving land that enslaves the devout and the profane without prejudice?

Perhaps it is the satisfaction of being able to make a living under such adverse conditions. Maybe it is the astonishing response of vegetation and livestock to a good rain, after months of drouth. These speculations seem pitifully inadequate, and it is probable that no native fully understands his strange willingness to be possessed by such demanding elements. But likely it is due in part to the people themselves, the natural gravitation of kindred personalities.

The early settlers—the ones who stayed—had many similar characteristics. The people, for the most part, were open, honest and friendly. They either liked or disliked you and would tell you so. All were industrious (imperative or they couldn't survive), had a sense of humor (a must to retain their sanity), and were adept at and gloried in the art of trading.

4

Ranchers would ride for miles and stay for days to help a neighbor out of a jam. But they would kill you on the spot for stealing a calf. Strange and backward fellows, these old-timers; if there was a thief or killer in their midst, they did not blame their honest friends and neighbors for his depredations —as our present society is now blamed by every do-gooder for the unlawful and malicious acts performed by its sullen dregs. The congenital misfit was held accountable for his own actions and dealt with accordingly.

A loving mother could not be more tenderly solicitous of her first-born than these hard-twisted cowboys were of a sick colt or calf. And like the protective mother they could be utterly savage if anything on the ranch was threatened. Daily, they would drive themselves, their hands, and their horses to the limits of their physical strength. Then after supper, filled with hot biscuits and fatigue, these worried cowmen might limp back and forth, gaze at the clear starlit sky, and curse the drouth or pray for rain, whichever was in keeping with their nature.

The strangest kinship of all became evident some years later. Oil was discovered in Winkler County in 1926, and there was a tremendous influx of all the personnel it takes to explore and produce an oil field. When the boom, or booms, began to die down the drifters moved on. The steadier hands who stayed are, oddly enough, endowed with much the same spirit, sense of value, and humor as the old-timers, despite the fact that their livelihood is in no way dependent upon the weather. This oddity, to a degree, supports the tenuous theory that terrain and climatic conditions tend to attract men of comparable character.

II

The eventful life of John Furman Haley began August 14, 1897, in Bell County, Texas. He was the third of six children born to John Alva and Julia Evetts Haley, though Burrett, his older brother, died before John was born. The remaining five, three girls and two boys, lived full and interesting lives. Indeed his younger brother Evetts—a man of considerable renown—spent some time in the saddle on his ninetieth birthday July 5, 1991.

These were restless times, or John's father (respectfully referred to as Papa by his children and later his grandchildren) was a restless man. When John was about three years old the family made the first of several moves west, to the small community of Norton in Runnels County.

From there they moved farther west to Sterling County, where Papa bought a small ranch and went into the cow business. In 1905 they backtracked to Miles in eastern Tom Green County, and John entered school. His teachers were not destined to be long-suffering, however, for later that same year Papa moved his growing brood to Roscoe in Nolan County. Only a few months were spent at this way station. In 1906 they moved to Midland, which would ultimately become the permanent home of Mama and Papa Haley. Since that time there has been an irregular ebb and flow of their children, grandchildren and great-grandchildren. Wonder what there is about Midland?

If John ever suffered from uncertainty and frustration it must have been during this time. Children are apt to aspire to the achievements of the adults close to them, and John must have been hard put to decide whether he wanted to run a hostelry, be a rancher, farmer, druggist, mortician, tax assessor, or operate a hardware store. There was no apparent limit to Papa's fields of endeavor; showing a profit was his goal, and the only restriction was honesty.

Papa had begun to settle down it seems. The family stayed in Midland five years before the next move, and John became acquainted with, though never reconciled to, the routine of primary education. Fortunately for him the tedium was broken by summer vacations. And in those days they weren't called back from an ever-shortening summer break to try out for this or practice for that. They had a full three months away from school.

He spent one summer, probably 1907 or 1908, with Uncle Russell Evetts on a farm near Fort Stockton. Uncle Russell, like Papa, was a disciplinarian.

"I remember hoeing weeds out of a peanut patch one afternoon," John reminisced. "I probably wasn't choppin' many weeds, but I was eatin' lots of peanuts. They sure were good. Directly Uncle Russell hollered across the small patch.

'John, are you eatin' those peanuts?'

'No sir.'

'Come here and let me look in your mouth.'

"Well, sir, I was always scared to death of Uncle Russell anyway and I sure did hate to go over there. I got about half way and he kinda grinned a little and said, 'Aw, go on back there and chop those weeds and be damn sure you don't eat any of those peanuts.'

8

'Yes sir.'

"Well, after that I chopped a lot more weeds and didn't eat any more peanuts—that day." It must have been rare good fortune to get a reprieve from Uncle Russell.

"The best thing about that summer, though, was Uncle Russell's mule colt. He follered us everywhere Uncle Russell'd let him, and that was just about everywhere. He'd even foller the wagon when Uncle Russell went to Midland. The mule would foller us to the fields and foller us back and he wouldn't let anybody walk between him and Uncle Russell. Well, I was always pickin' at him. I'd sneak around and get between them, and he'd run me off. Then I'd wait until he stopped to get a bite or two of grass and I'd slip between them again, and he'd run me off again. He'd damn sure run you off too, bitin' and kickin' both. I sure enjoyed that mule colt."

John would have pitied today's unfortunate children with their neat uniforms, fine playgrounds, competent coaching, and no spontaneous fun. How much more exciting to match speed and agility with the quarrelsome colt. Not bad training, either; he learned early on that some of life's games will never be governed by a fair and impartial referee.

Late in 1909 Papa bought a ranch in northwestern Loving County. The Pecos River was the boundary on the west, New Mexico on the north, and the house was located within a few hundred yards of Pope's Crossing. The ranch was operated by Uncle Durward, one of Papa's brothers, who had an interest in this venture. They kept the place only two years, but the two summers John spent there—the last one in company with his brother Evetts—might have had a great deal to do with the life he chose.

Though barely in his teens when the ranch was sold, John's experiences there were so memorable that he could and did relate them in graphic detail throughout his lifetime. And Evetts, four years younger, still has vivid recollections.

The conditions were ideal. The Ezells, across the river, had a large horse ranch and from time to time bunches of mares and colts would stray over on Papa's place. Rounding up wild mares is not an exercise recommended for serious-minded or timid men, but for carefree reckless youths it is great sport. Also, the Ezells were good hands and congenial neighbors, so nothing could have been better from John's youthful point of view. But there was more. There was Uncle Durward, neither an unyielding disciplinarian nor a demanding taskmaster. He was a lovable man with an endless fund of stories. Hence, when Papa wasn't around, the boys were handled with a lighter quirt and looser rein. For John, energetic and exuberant, and Evetts, zestful and imaginative, this must have been close to heaven. No wonder the fond and enduring memories.

During the second summer Uncle Durward, John, and Evetts were building several miles of fence. When they decided to call it a day and make camp, John was told to unhitch the team and take them to water. He probably complied with alacrity for it was a half mile down a cross fence to water, and Evetts was stuck with the uninspiring chores of gathering wood, greasing the wagon, filling the lantern, etc. John hung the harness on the wagon, slipped a lead rope over the head of the off horse, hopped on the old mare bareback, and set out. The mare was apparently gentle and no one seemed to know what caused her to run away.

When a horse runs away there isn't much anyone can do, and there are few things a rider had rather not see in front of him than a barbed wire fence. An amazing number of things run through the mind at such a time. "Should I quit him? Will he stop? Will he turn down the fence, go straight over it, or worst of all, hit it at an angle?" John elected to stay with the mare, and she must have hit the fence at an angle, for he suffered a terrible cut between the knee and ankle, going to the bone. (Daddy told me years later that the mare was so badly

cut she bled to death in a matter of minutes.)

This was to be the first of many experiences with runaway teams, for in December 1911 Papa sold the ranch and shortly after bought an irrigated farm in eastern Tom Green County near Miles. There were over 600 acres under irrigation out of the Concho, and they worked it with horses and mules.

"When we quit for the day," Daddy recalled, "we usually left our equipment in the field. We would unhitch, put a halter on each horse or mule in the four-up teams, then neck them together with a rope running from halter to halter. The driver would always ride the near horse.

"We were comin' in one afternoon about dusk. A Mexican named Manuel was in the lead; next came Scott, with a team of horses, and I was in the rear ridin' Old Jim, a sorrel mule. About halfway to the barn a bunch of hogs ran across the road and boogered the lead team. They whirled and took off, as did Scott's. But Scott's team was a little slow and the Mexican's team ran right up astraddle of them. Old Jim, seein' what was comin', wheeled like a cuttin' horse, poppin' that off mule around like the end of a whip, and the race was on. It was about 500 yards to where the fence turned west. My team made the turn and stayed together 'til they quit; but the others busted up. One black mare ran over two or three fences and one mule came in with nothin' on but the collar. Scott was scared to death. We later heard him tellin' his wife, 'Why, I could feel Manuel's halter ropes rubbin' across my back.' We were always havin' runaways down there. Hell, the damned mules would run away just for the fun of it."

The summers at the ranch had been great fun and no doubt John regretted the move to Tom Green County, but he was soon deeply immersed in the operation of the farm. This would soon turn into a full-time job, for shortly after entering the eighth grade, John quit school.

Modern educational customs virtually petition for comment on Papa's wisdom in permitting such a move. In this age of unreasoning, almost frantic insistence that all children, regardless of intellectual bent or inclination, should not only finish high school but continue through the institutions of higher learning, Papa's judgement would seem to be in question. John, however, was what is now popularly referred to as a physical man. He had no interest in theories, philosophy, or problems in the abstract. He was concerned only with tangibles, preferably those close to home. Driven by an unbelievable source of energy, John could not at the time—nor was he ever able to—sit still long enough to enjoy the delights of Shakespeare, Cervantes, Homer and Conrad. But he could be enthralled for hours at a time searching through the bowels of a piece of intricate machinery for the worn or broken part that had caused a malfunction. To force such a boy through school would have been "cruel and unusual punishment" and would have accomplished nothing, for learning is of value only if earnestly sought and assiduously applied. Papa knew his son well.

John was not a piddler as are many "fix-it" men. He liked to work, but he wanted to see something accomplished—and in the shortest possible time. This is probably where he started his policy of making many repairs at night so the whole crew would not be delayed the next day. His temperament and energy often brought to mind a whirlwind in a branding pen, and he sometimes stirred up just as much dust.

Nowadays, with modern equipment, a farm of over 600 acres can be worked with very little manpower. But in 1912, the operation required several steady hands and a corral full of workhorses. John was put to work full-time with grown men and was expected to pull his share of the load. This proved to be no obstacle as he showed remarkable aptitude for all phases of farming, and by the time Papa sold the place John was considered a top hand.

He was developing quickly from a boy to a man, but some time in 1914 during their last year on the farm, he was firmly reminded that this milestone had not yet been reached. John let his ever-present temper so impair his judgement that he actually talked back to Papa! Telling the story years later he said: "The first thing that hit the floor was the back of my head, and Papa taught me damn quick that I wasn't near old enough nor big enough to be arguing with him."

"Papa was sitting astraddle of John, and I was squalling bloody murder," Evetts recalls, "when Papa looked over his shoulder and commanded, 'Dry up, Evetts.' And I dried up."

The incident also served as a lesson to the rest of the children and must have made quite an impression. To this day many recollections are dated from "the argument."

January 1, 1915, Papa traded the Concho River farm to H. Emil Schumm for eleven sections in arid Loving County, and the family moved back to Midland—this time to stay.

Papa, always a man of remarkable astuteness, took advantage of the train service, leaving Mama Haley and the children to cope with the infuriating vagaries of the Model T.

Soon after settling in their new home, John went to work as a repairman for the Midland Hardware Company. The well-equipped shop and thriving business provided a challenging outlet for his enormous energies. Most of his work pertained to windmills and related parts and accessories such as pump-jacks and engines which were used to provide water for thirsty cattle when the much-maligned wind decided to teach everyone a lesson by refusing to blow.

For the benefit of those not conversant with ranch operations, this particular aspect should perhaps be clarified. There is a wide area of West Texas where a rancher's sole supply of water is furnished by windmills. When his range is lightly stocked, has adequate water reserves and the wind blows faithfully, his problems are slight. Keeping the waterings in

14

good repair is the only requirement. But, when the grass is good, the ranges carrying a maximum number of cattle, the wells weak and far apart, it is a different story. Particularly when the wind doesn't cooperate.

When this happens the mill is cut off and a pump-jack and engine are set up to take its place. A cowboy sometimes runs two or three engines day and night and also has to look after the cattle around these waterings. This is a sorry time for cowboys, most of them neither mentally nor tempermentally suited for the job. They have spent their lives learning the art of working cattle and have not had the time nor the slightest inclination to study the mysteries of the gasoline engine.

These devilish contraptions pose no problem at all for a mechanic, but in the minds of most cowboys the combustion engine is a mysterious manifestation of evil, designed by some clever, vengeful demon who is fixated with albatrosses and has vowed to spend eternity tormenting hapless riders. That these instruments of torture have other uses is just a fortuitous accident.

The cowboy feels betrayed. Winter and spring when he would like a little peace and quiet the wind moans and wails incessantly. Now, here it is late summer, fall coming on, the cattle are fat and the horses anxious to work, and when he cuts the engine off to fill it with gas and grease it, there is nothing but silence. Especially silent windmills! The capricious wind perversely refuses to turn a leaf, let alone a mill. Small wonder that cowboys believe the wind is feminine in gender, and small wonder that Midland Hardware was booming. John's services were much in demand. There were shop repairs, and he was often sent to ranches to set up and repair engines on the spot. Occasionally he was sent to waterings fifty miles away and even farther just to get one started.

He stayed with this job for eleven months, and the experience was invaluable, but late spring in 1916, Papa stocked

15

the Loving County ranch with approximately 190 head of Hereford and Durham cattle and sent John to look after it.

III

Evetts joined John at the ranch when school was out. They built some corrals at what was then called the North Mill and broke some of the forty or fifty broncs Papa acquired in the Schumm trade.

Two great cow horses were to come out of that bunch: a big grey named Hammer and his half brother Keno, a light-bodied, rough-traveling blue. Keno was gentle as a puppy, but Hammer would pitch every now and then as long as he lived. "He didn't pitch far but he was hard to ride," John used to say. "As a rule he would pitch like hell for eight or ten jumps then turn straight back, and if he didn't get you he would quit." Through the years Hammer acquired quite a reputation as a cow horse and pitching horse. He had a peculiar twist that would often shoot a man straight up so that he hit the ground on his feet. This is sort of like jumping off the roof of a shed, but it is quite a bit better than diving off.

When I was old enough to hold onto the saddle strings, and Hammer was showing signs of mellowing in his advanced age, Daddy would sometimes put me behind the saddle and take me along. This was always a great time, and at first no thought was given to what horse we were riding. But I was raised on a steady diet of stories about Hammer and his victims, and one day as we were loping along it occurred to me that he might throw us off. Visions of landing on the bottom and being squashed by Daddy were paramount. Idle questions were never encouraged, but as this unsettling scenario grew in my mind, the more convinced I became that this frightening possibility had not occurred to my father and that it should be brought to his attention.

"Daddy, what will we do if ol' Hammer throws us off?" I asked. But due to the wind and the squeaking saddle he didn't understand me. He loped a little farther then pulled up to a slow easy trot.

"What did you say?" he asked over his shoulder.

"I was just wondering what we would do if ol' Hammer throws us off?" was the timid reply.

"Then, by God, we'll walk. Now shut up and quit asking so many questions." That, of course, took care of what we would do, but it did nothing to dispel my dread of landing on the bottom.

Whoa, this is getting way ahead of the story. We've got to backtrack to the time when Daddy and Hammer were both broncs—back to 1916 to be specific.

Apparently that was a good year. But the ranch was heavily stocked and John was soon to become well acquainted with the hazards of overstocking West Texas range. There was practically no rain throughout 1917 and by the end of summer all the grass was gone. Several ranchers—John included—found some pasturage near Barstow, about twenty miles southwest of the ranch. The small farms in this area were irrigated out of the Pecos River by means of a network of canals. One of the principal crops was alfalfa, and it was to this scanty growth that the drouth-stricken ranchers trailed herds.

John moved Papa's cattle early that fall. When he got them located and settled, he went back to help W. F.

Scarborough, a neighbor to the north, move a herd of cows and calves to the Barstow farms.

"It was a hell of a drive," John recalled years later. "The cattle were poor and weak, and there were a good many baby calves. On top of that Mr. Scarborough was shorthanded. It was slow going all the way, but I remember one day in particular. We made such a short distance that when we made camp that night we were still in sight of the bedgrounds of the night before.

"I remember one other thing about that drive. We were about halfway to Barstow, I guess, and the herd was scattered and strung out a good ways. The cattle were pickin' at that dry grass stubble and movin' as slow as if they were on grass knee-high. Most of the calves had fallen to the rear like they always do after they've been on the move two or three days, and the boys bringin' up the drags were havin' hell. Those baby calves would walk a ways then lay down. The drag hands would get 'em up and started again, then turn off to push some more along; then the first calves'd lay down again. One of the men was sure havin' trouble. One little calf was takin' all his time. He couldn't leave him for a minute to do anything else, and the drags were gettin' further behind. Finally he got so disgusted that when the calf laid down again, he just rode off and left him. He thought he was safe because the boss was way up front on the point. But old Bill Scarborough was a real cowman, and he saw everything. He was back there in just a little bit and that puncher sure got his packin' eat out. When the old man got through chewin' him out he told him to go back and get that calf. 'If he can't walk, carry him,' he hollered. And that was the way we did it. Drive 'em as far as they'd go, then carry 'em. Sometimes we'd carry 'em up about the middle of the herd and set 'em down. Then go back and get another one. I sure was glad when that drive was over."

The move to Barstow was barely worthwhile. Under favorable conditions alfalfa is good pasturage, but that year the cattle went in at the end of the growing season, the pickings were slim, and the fields were grazed off in very short order. There were a lot of cattle in the country in 1917, and the Pecos River farms near Barstow cover a relatively small area. Therefore it is easy to imagine that for every cow they could pasture, there were a hundred more needing it.

Such conditions, not unnaturally, tempted some less than honest but plenty gutsy cowmen to supplement their inadequate pasture by turning cattle into their neighbors' fields at night, despite the fact that some of the pastures were patrolled by armed riders. "They must have been pretty damned well organized," John declared, "for sometimes I'd find as many as fifty head of cattle near an open gate that I'd been by less than an hour before, and I never did catch anybody." Since he was denied the pleasure of dealing with the culprits themselves, he contented himself with the next most satisfying thing: the cowboy's favorite sport of roping as many strays as he can comfortably catch while throwing them out of his pasture. "When I was ridin' ol' Hammer I'd fairground 'em," John laughed. "He was big and stout with pretty good speed and he could sure lay one down. One night I'd caught five or six off of him and he was workin' awful good. I was after another one and was just fixin' to throw when the steer boogered at somethin' and turned right back by me. When ol' Hammer ducked back after 'im, he slipped down. After that he wouldn't run any more that night. I could get 'im into a little slow lope but he wouldn't run atall. The next time I rode 'im he was alright though."

The meager grazing didn't last long, and late in December John and Evetts moved the cattle back home. The trail outfit consisted of John, Evetts and a neighbor's son, J. D. Magee, who was saddled with the chore of making a Model-T serve as a chuck wagon.

The afternoon before reaching the ranch they penned at Ward Wells, about five or six miles southwest of the Schumm place. They fed the horses, ate supper, and decided to spend the night with the Nelsons, an old couple who lived in a little frame house about four miles to the northwest.

"This was December 26, 1917," Evetts recalled. "I was out of school for Christmas vacation and—gee it was cold! The Nelsons had already gone to bed, but they got up and welcomed us and said we could roll our beds out on the porch.

"'We'll help you with bedding,'" they said.

"They went into the house and came out with a feather mattress. That old Magee boy got down on it and whispered ecstatically: "Look at it—a feather mattress!"

"We drained the water out of the car by the light of a full moon to keep it from freezing, as we did every night, fixed our beds on the borrowed mattress and, as it was getting late, quickly settled down for the night."

This voluptuous comfort would be short-lived, for John misread the hands on his watch and rousted them out early. Real early. "Ten minutes after six!" he roared. "The damned alarm didn't go off!"

"We hurriedly rolled our beds and loaded them," Evetts said. "Then John got the old Ford started. The sky had become overcast and it was dark as the dickens. We stumbled over everything on the place carrying water and the manifold was red hot before we got the radiator filled. Safer to do it this way though, because those old cars weren't too reliable, and if you filled them with water first, they might freeze up before you could get them started. Damn, I'm glad somebody finally invented antifreeze. Ready at last, we jumped in and hightailed it south to Ward Wells.

"When we got there we fixed breakfast, saddled the horses, and it still wasn't breaking day. We gathered more wood and moved closer to the fire, turning round and round, roasting

21

first one side, then the other, wondering why the hell it didn't get light. Oh, man, it was cold!

"The clouds were breaking away and a good many stars showing, but it was still dark as could be. So we assumed the moon had gone down. But hell! If the moon was down, it should be getting light in the east. Something was wrong! About that time someone looked up and saw a little sliver of the moon showing way up in the sky, where it had no business being that time of day. As we watched, more and more of the moon became exposed, and we realized for the first time that there had been a total eclipse. But the moon was still out of place; it wasn't even near the horizon. We looked at John accusingly, and he dug out his watch and held it in the firelight. The hands pointed to 4:30. It had one of those radium dials, and when John looked at it in the dark at the Nelson's house he mistook 2:30 for ten minutes after six. John was mad at himself, and J. D. and I were just as mad. I've never had any use for radium dial watches since then."

Moving a herd of poor cattle shorthanded is frustrating enough. But subjecting your help to all the pitfalls inherent in the use of modern gadgets can lead to bloody noses. John was lucky.

All those handicaps notwithstanding, they did manage to get the cattle back to the ranch—back to eleven sections of grazed-off barren country. From here on till grass started in the spring—provided there was enough winter and spring moisture to start the grass—there would be prayer, sweat and cottonseed cake, a lot of each.

Feeding cattle through the winter at that time on very short grass or none at all was an uphill job, but selling them was out of the question. Ranchers had to ship by rail to the nearest market in Fort Worth, and the only buyers for cattle in this miserable condition were the packers. Canner cows did not bring much money. The cowman, on occasion, would gamble too long on the possibility of rain, and when it didn't come the cattle were too weak to stand the trip to Fort Worth. Such was the case in 1917. There was no extra grass within trailing distance, and there were no cattle trucks then to haul livestock to distant grassland, even if it could be found. There was no option. Feed them or lose them. A lot of cake was fed that winter, and the ranchers troubles were compounded in January 1918 by one of the worst blizzards in the history of the country.

Nowadays, you can sit in the living room and watch some television weatherman, with benefit of the meteorologist's charts and satellites, trace the path of a storm from its point of origin to its ultimate dissipation. Back then the first warning was when the leading edge of clouds rushed over the northern horizon.

John went to Pyote that day to get a load of cake, leaving Mama Haley, who had come out from Midland to stay a few days, at the ranch.

"I left Pyote about three o'clock in the afternoon as I recall," John said, "and the clouds were just comin' in sight. I ran into the wind about three or four miles out of town and by the time I got to Hookedy—a watering five miles north of Pyote—it was already spittin' snow. Damn that thing came in fast. It was almost unbelievable. About a mile north of Hookedy I passed one of Scarborough's men who'd left town about an hour ahead of me. He had a wagon-load of feed and groceries and a good four-horse team pullin' it. But he was already havin' trouble with 'em. It was so cold and the wind was blowin' the snow into their faces so hard that they could hardly stand it.

"Our roads in those days were just two shallow ruts made by wagons meanderin' through the scattered bushes, and when the snow got deep enough to fill the ruts everything looked alike. Before I got to Threes—another watering six or seven miles northwest of Hookedy—the road was gettin' hard to follow. The next watering ahead was known as Twos, and a camp was there. It was about five miles northwest of Threes. And that was a long, tough five miles. Dark caught me right after I left Threes, and drivin' with my head out the window tryin' to make those dim headlights follow those two winding trails was a mean job.

"The going got slower and tougher. The snow piled up 'til it kept stalling my Model-T, and I was havin' to back up and take runs at it by the time I reached Twos. I wanted to stay there 'til morning, but I was gettin' more and more worried about Mama bein' at the ranch in that old drafty shack by herself. One of the Mooreheads was stayin' at the Twos camp and he helped me tie some ropes around my wheels to give some traction. I took off again. It was only about three miles on up to my camp, and I thought maybe I could make  it. But I didn't get three hundred yards before the ropes cut out, so I spent the night with Moorehead after all. Next morning we managed to catch a horse, and I pulled out for the ranch—still worried about Mama.

"I should have known better. Mama had everything under control. The only thing that was botherin' her was a baby calf. She had carried him into the shack and put him in a box behind the old wood stove, but he still froze to death.

"I found out later that Scarborough's man, Bill Russell I think it was, had gone all the way to their Hardland camp, twenty miles north of where I last saw him, that same night. So he had quite a trip. He blindfolded his team with tow sacks so they could face that blowin' snow and somehow managed to follow the road and just kept goin'. Had to walk most of the

24

way of course to keep from freezin'. It's a damned wonder he didn't trip over a bush and fall under the wagon wheels."

We might dwell a little longer on the Scarborough cowboy's determination and endurance. It seems a little unfair to dismiss him on the note of his good fortune at not being crushed under the wheels of the wagon.

Fighting your way into a howling blizzard for only a few hundred yards can be a terrifying experience. That anyone could do it for twenty miles defies reason. Breathing is arduous. The extreme cold so saps the strength and numbs the senses that coherent thought becomes difficult. That cowboy not only had to force his team to face the arctic wind and cutting snow, he had to keep track of the road, since his blindfolded horses could not.

What motivated the Scarborough hand that terrible night? It was only a few miles back to Pyote, and the wind would have been at his back. There were two ranch houses between Hookedy and his destination, each less than a mile off his route. Why not take shelter and deliver his load the following day? What, if anything, was in the wagon to lend such compelling urgency? The cowboy himself might not have given a satisfactory answer. Yet I ask myself these unanswerable questions over and over—and feel ashamed. Must heroics always be logically explained?

Considering the condition of the cattle and the severity of the storm, the ranchers suffered a relatively light death loss. But the storm took its toll in flesh and strength, both of which the cattle that had managed to survive the drouth could ill afford to lose.

John, however, by virtue of feeding heavily and regularly and by "tailing up" the weaker cows, managed to make it through the winter. Due to improved roads and transportation and the proximity of many cattle auctions, the frustrating, back-breaking work of "tailing up" cows "on the lift" is a thing of the past, and nobody yearns for its return.

25

"On the lift" means that when a cow lies down, she is unable to get back on her feet without help. If she is not "tailed up" the cow will die on the spot from cold and/or starvation. In order to accomplish this task, the cowboy squats behind the cow, then passes her tail across the back of his neck as far as he can—especially if he is not very tall. Then he tries to spook her so she will make an effort to get to her feet. When she makes the effort, so does he, and how. If the cow is already exhausted from previous efforts, then the cowboy has to lift much more weight. He strains with every ounce of strength, his eyes bug out, his chest pounds, and his head swims. Then he finds that her rump has to be two inches higher to enable her to get her hind feet in position, so he lets her down, gets a shorter hold on the tail, and goes through the same routine again. Just as he is about to faint, she takes a little of the weight with her back legs, then shakily one leg at a time, she gets up on her front feet and, thank God, she is standing, trembling and unsteady but nevertheless on her feet.

Now the cowboy starts backing slowly away, being careful not to disturb her until her circulation and equilibrium have returned to normal. Old, weak cows are similar to a good many aged and infirm humans—they are irritable and suspicious. She sees the cowboy trying to slink cowardly away and instantly decides that this intruder, this violator of "animal rights," is not going to get away this time. So she wheels to charge—and falls down again. By this time he is weak and shaky himself; he carries water and feed to her, loudly and profanely consigns her soul to everlasting hell, then comes back in an hour or so and tries again.

This "romance of the range" is what occupied the "dashing" cowboys of the Southwest through the winter of 1917 and 1918. Spring came at last, but there still had been no moisture of consequence. The January snow had helped some but not enough, so in June Papa decided to move everything to his property southwest of Midland called the Young place. Evetts was again out of school and anxious to start his "vacation," but they needed at least one more man. John went to Pyote and asked his friend, Fitz Sitton, to help them for a few days. After John's death, Mr. Sitton repeated this conversation:

"Aw, John, it won't do no good. We won't do nothin' but fight, and we won't never get any work done."

"Hell, Fitz. I've got to have some help. Maybe we can work everything in."

"Alright, if you think we can do it."

And so they did. The three young men gathered the cattle into the shipping pens at Pyote, shaped them up and loaded them on the cars. The cattle cars were picked up by an eastbound freight, and John's long fight with the drouth was over.

On July 5th, John and Evetts went to El Paso, where John joined the Army, and the Navy rejected Evetts.

"Too small and too young," they told the disconsolate youngster.

A pity the services are so inflexible. They avidly accept a given tonnage and longevity and steadfastly ignore the invaluable qualities of intelligence, desire and spirit. Be that as it may, Evetts went back home—and John wound up in France.

IV

John was in the Army only nine months, and though he went overseas, he arrived too late to see any action. He was sent from Fort Bliss to Gettysburg, Pennsylvania, and from there to Scranton. On September 25, 1918, his outfit shipped out from New York. It was some trip.

The troop transport was an old English ship named *Saxon*. She was said to have carried British troops during the Boer War, and according to John she might still have been serving food from those same supplies. "Rotten and wormy" was the way he described it. Furthermore, as is common with troopships, she was packed.

Those are familiar conditions to every serviceman who has shipped overseas. Diarrhea, upset stomach, seasickness and the inevitable loss of vitality are expected conditions. However, these troops were not to be let off so easily. Shortly after sailing, hundreds of men came down with influenza, John included. His case was milder than some, and he was up and around before they reached England.

Bad weather added to their miseries. "It was rough all the way across," John said. "But we were hit by a real storm in the Irish Sea. The thing hit all of a sudden. Some of us were in the mess hall when we felt an awful jolt; there was dead calm for maybe half a minute and at first we thought we'd been hit by a torpedo. In fact, one big fellow jumped up and ran for the ladder hollerin', 'She's settlin! She's settlin!' He got about halfway up when another big wave hit and a solid stream of water came pourin' through the hatch and somersaulted him back down."

Though he was probably more aware than most of nature's tempestuous whims and awesome power, this was John's only experience with a storm at sea and his stories about it were interesting. Unfortunately, I am unable to repeat many of them—the details are much too hazy. They were descriptive but often disjointed and were related a long time ago. Although the ensuing account is my phraseology it conveys the essence of John's recollections.

As the *Saxon* pitched and rolled in the mountainous seas, the lower decks became a sickening mess. Several hundred men were lying in makeshift wards, many of them virtually helpless. There was no warning, no time to secure the men in their bunks, if indeed that were possible. The nurses and medics went about their tasks over slippery, wildly tilting decks amidst cries of delirium from the critical cases. Curses and whining demands from the not-so-seriously ill pounded their ears as they stubbornly grappled with an impossible situation. While inhaling the stench of excrement, vomit, sweat and fear, they organized clean-up crews, took temperatures and dispensed medication. Neither medical personnel nor the patients knew, or much cared, about what was happening topside. Their own lot was too miserable.

The old ship was taking water and most of the men aboard thought she would sink any minute. It was to be hours, however, before the *Saxon* was forced to break radio silence. Fortunately it was a British destroyer, not a German submarine, that pulled alongside. But there was nothing she could do. She couldn't take the *Saxon* in tow or transfer men—the seas were too rough. The destroyer could only stand off and watch as the floundering troopship fought her way through huge battering waves to the safety of Mersey estuary. The collective sigh of relief was probably heard over the roar of the wind, for it was relatively smooth sailing from there to the protected harbor at Liverpool, England.

Weak, seasick, homesick, and just plain sick, the soldiers who could walk shouldered full packs and rifles and went ashore. John recalled that several hundred were carried off on stretchers and there were some who did not make it to England. "I never knew how many men died," he said, "but I'd guess about thirty-five were buried at sea."

From the dock, the troops had to negotiate a long steep hill to reach their quarters. They were glad to be there, but the imposing hill was a test of endurance. As the men labored up the grade under sixty-pound packs, trying to adjust their faltering steps to the solid soil of England after the violently rolling decks of the *Saxon*, they were joined by English children who were bent upon testing the generosity of American soldiers. Not yet fully recovered from the flu and certainly not in the best of moods, John misunderstood a local lad's plaintive plea for "cents, cents" and summarily snapped: "Don't have any sense or I wouldn't be here." Many years later he ruefully confessed, "When it finally soaked in on me that the kid was begging for pennies, I felt kind of bad."

From Liverpool John's outfit went to Winchester, England, and then to Southhampton where they loaded out to cross the Channel. They landed in Le Havre, France, a few days before the war was over. John was in a replacement tank company—Company D, 344th Battalion—but the armistice was signed before his company was sent to the front.

He shipped out from Marseilles, France, March 1, 1919, on a French ship named *Patricia*, and once again most of those aboard got sick, this time not so seriously.

31

"That old round-bottomed boat just rocked and rolled," John said. "All the troops and half the crew got seasick. We didn't even have any toilet paper 'til we got to Gibraltar.

"We landed in New York, March 17th—St. Patrick's Day. They took us to Camp Mills on Long Island where we got a couple days furlough. From there we went to Camp Mead, Maryland, where we got another furlough, and I went to Washington, D. C. to see a relative named Ezra Grimes."

The army finally made up its mind and sent John to Camp Owen, a base near Boerne, Texas. He was discharged April 9, 1919, which immediately made him a private in those legions of footloose young men who are so noticeable after every major war. People mistakenly believe that the ex-soldiers' nomadic behavior for those next few years is a result of traumatic war experiences. In reality, as they are no longer hobbled by military discipline or parental authority, the returning veterans are merely responding to a very natural yen that has been with them since early adolescence—the compelling urge to see something of the world on their own. John had all the normal impulses.

Arriving back in Midland, he found that the drouth had not broken, so he went to Breckenridge and found a job dressing tools in the oil field. He took to this work like a milk cow to flower beds. Everything was interesting. In those days, oil-field hands worked twelve-hour shifts, but John believed twelve idle hours in one day were a sinful waste, so he found a second job: firing boilers at a nearby rig.

"Was that also a twelve hour shift?" I asked years later.

"Yeah, but I had a lot of time to sleep there. It really wasn't too hard to hold down both jobs."

The next few months found John working at various jobs around Breckenridge. He was on a casing crew in Young County, drove a service car for a while, and generally made an oil-field hand until the spring of 1920.

Nothing is known of what he did besides work. The only hint is in a letter John wrote to Papa during this period. It was a typical dutiful-letter-home except for this closing remark: "The wife of one of the roughnecks lives near here and she is a good sport. I may be getting in trouble." There is no record of whether or not he got in trouble, but there was a great deal of fretting back home.

The work was enjoyable. And high-salaried jobs were easy to find. John also enjoyed the comfortable feeling that envelops a man when he knows his proficiency enables him to choose work that appeals to his needs or fancies. Another attraction to his adventurous spirit was the carefree, boisterous camaraderie of a boom town. John, no doubt, was well satisfied with the state of the world and his own position in it. But then...? Then came spring.

A cowboy is hard to wean from the country, and for some reason the spring of the year is the most difficult. When he is away from his horse and saddle he does not recall the cold dry winters and even drier springs. A puncher's memory conveniently deletes the suffocating dust and blinding sandstorms, the helpless rage and frustration when riding crazy, cold-jawed horses while driving slow-moving herds of weak cows and baby calves. He remembers instead all the good things.

A rider thinks of cool, crisp mornings, yearns for the smell of burning mesquite and an unobstructed view of the heavens at night. In his daydreams, the displaced cowboy pulls on his boots, rolls up his bed and can almost feel the damp stiff tarp. He inhales the delightful odor of frying bacon, remembers the tingling excitement of saddling an unknown bronc before daylight, and revels in the exhilaration of "fitting" a good ride on a hard-pitching horse. The creak of the saddle on a favorite mount, the jingle of spurs and feel of a rope, cattle on the mend, and the promise of rain are magnetic forces that few cowboys can long resist. Certainly John could not. He came back to Midland in the spring and probably helped Papa deliver what cattle were left from the Young place, southwest of town. Then in late spring or early summer, he started punching cows west of the Pecos River.

He worked on a ranch north of Van Horn for a short while, then for Elmer Jones, a great cowboy, who ranched southeast of Pecos. "Elmer Jones was one of the best cowpunchers I ever knew," John once said. "He knew how to handle cattle and made quite a name for himself as a roper. He could ride anything that had hair on it, and it was all fun.

"There were five or six big Mexican steers on his place that were strays. They were seven or eight years old and weighed around 1100 pounds. Old Elmer never would throw 'em out; he'd just rope 'em every time it came handy. He'd forefoot one, jerk 'im down, then ride up and give 'im slack so he could get up. That way he never would have to get off his horse. One day though, when he rode up to turn one loose, the rope slipped off one front foot and drew up around the other one. He jerked 'im down again and I got off my horse to take it off. I got a tail-hold and pulled the rope off his foot and Elmer hollered…."

'Ride 'im!'

'Hell, I don't want to ride 'im. Ride 'im yourself!'

'Hold 'im!'

"He jumped off his horse and stepped astraddle the steer. I handed him the tail, and the show was on. That old steer came up so fast that it almost seemed like he started pitching from flat on his side. Elmer rode 'im twenty or thirty steps lookin' back over his shoulder grinnin' and then stepped off.

He sure made it look easy.

"Most of Elmer's horses would pitch and some were hard to ride. I had one in my mount that would also rear up and fall back once in a while. Most of the time, he'd pitch a few jumps, then rear up and just keep comin' up and back until you'd decide to get down. When he felt you loosen, he'd come back down pitchin' and buck you off. If he didn't buck you off, he'd usually have you off balance, which would make 'im that much harder to ride.

"We were prowlin' for worms one mornin' after a shower and I was ridin' this horse. He had already pitched a couple of times and I was about winded, for it was all I could do to stay on him. Besides, he was gettin' worse about that rearin' up. We were trottin' down a fence line, and I was hopin' he was done for the day when he 'broke in two' again. This time, though, he hadn't made over three or four jumps before he hit a slick spot and fell. He came back up pitchin' and just bucked round and round, right over the top of me. All I could hear was Elmer laughin'. He finally got the horse off to one side and caught 'im. Then he called back, still laughin',

'Did he hurt you?'

'Naw, never touched me.'

'Ha ha ha, I thought he was steppin' on you every jump. Let me have 'im awhile,' Elmer said.

'Alright.'

"Elmer walked over to the fence and took out a heavy cedar stay. He broke off about two feet of the butt end and got on that horse without changing saddles. My stirrups were way too short for him, and he looked sorta' funny trottin' along with his knees up to the swell of the saddle, wavin' the heavy end of that fence stay around and lookin' plumb unconcerned about everything.

"Sure enough, we hadn't gone a half mile before that rearin'-up son-of-a-gun broke in two again. And sure enough he hadn't made over four or five jumps 'til he reared right straight up. The only difference was that it wasn't me on him this time. Old Elmer just sorta' slid over to one side, put his left hand on the horse's neck and hit 'im three times over the eye with that stay. Man, he really hit 'im, too! Far as I know that horse never did rear up again. He sure made it look easy."

John, however, was doing something to earn his wages besides riding and roping, as is evidenced by this portion of a postcard mailed to Evetts, July 29, 1920:

"I am working by the month for Jones. Building fence more than anything else. But you tell the world I'm not doing much. I don't believe in hard work." Fiction was never John's long suit—ask anyone who ever worked with him—and a more pitiful effort than Evetts' postcard has probably never come to light.

Meanwhile, John, blissfully unaware of the consternation his message would eventually create, quit Elmer Jones and went to work at the Dixieland Ranch. L. W. Anderson owned the outfit and Nick Newel was running the wagon. Nick was middle-aged, small, weather-beaten and a native of the Pecos country. Maybe they were short of horses, Nick's cowboy sense of humor was working overtime, or he was irritated with John. Whatever the reason, he cut John a whole mount of broncs—not a gentle horse in the bunch. The horses were five- and six-year-olds, but they had only been ridden a few saddles, then turned out.

When the wagon pulled in, Mr. Anderson sent John to look after the cattle on a ranch southwest of Dixie.

"I packed my bed on one of the horses, a camping outfit on another and drove them across to this other place," John said. "When I got there, I found out there wasn't any horse pasture. There were fifty sections, and it was all one pasture. There wasn't even a corral. Lucky for me, I had been out with the wagon, so my horses were used to being caught in a rope corral. I hobbled them all and put one on a stake rope. And that's the way I handled them from then on. I always had one horse on a stake rope. I stayed there until sometime in December and never got left afoot.

"Then they moved me to the headquarters over east of the river, several miles northwest of Pyote. My horses were about used up, and I got a fresh mount when I got over there. But extra horses on a big outfit are never much good, so as soon as my horses rested up I took them back. Those old extras were as good as they were ever gonna be, and my broncs were gettin' better every day."

John quit the Anderson outfit in June 1921 and went to work for Papa at the Haley Hotel in Midland. He stayed there until February 1922, then went back to the oil fields at Breckenridge.

The fact that he worked in the hotel from June until February may seem a bit unusual to those who knew him, for John's boiling point—especially in his younger days—was extremely low. Furthermore, when in the midst of one of his frequent rages, he had a deplorable habit of breaking things—items such as windows, shovel handles, heads, doors, cook-stoves and teeth. Surely this sort of thing was bad for the hotel business!

Perhaps the guests flocked in to see the show, or maybe they were merely tolerant and long-suffering—though this seems unlikely. Of course, they did not always witness those colorful scenes. Once, for example, John was removing some custard pies from an oven. He was carefully sliding the pies out of the oven onto the open oven door to let them cool. This worked fine until a pie pan came in contact with the protruding head of a rivet and stopped. That is, the pie pan stopped, but the bubbling custard kept coming right over on the oven door—and his hand. This so infuriated him that he kicked the oven door as hard as he could, thereby decorating a large portion of the kitchen with fresh custard pie. No wonder he went back to Breckenridge; it must be awful to make a living cleaning custard pie off floors, ceilings, walls and cabinets.

This time John resisted the beckoning lure of the seductive cow country until June. He even lasted through the spring, proof that the oil field emits a powerful attraction of its own. Maybe it was higher wages, bright lights, the vivid recollection of a hotel kitchen, or "good-time" women; whatever the reason, he worked around Breckenridge until Papa decided to stock the ranch again.

V

Rain at last: the drouth, which began in 1917, finally broke in 1922, and Papa Haley restocked the Loving County ranch. That was in June, and John, apparently with no regrets, tore himself away from the seething activity of the Breckenridge boom and caught the next train headed west. The nesting instinct, even in a man, can be strong; he devoted the rest of his life to the care and growth of this ranch.

A cowboy living alone, unencumbered by barking dogs and predatory housecats, can observe the habits and peculiarities of the area's wildlife in its natural habitat, except around his camp, where waste grain scattered by horses, meat bones, and table scraps supplement nature's provisions. The animals and birds become curious, bold, and ultimately dependent upon these morsels. Like the American people, wild things are unable to perceive the perilous risk inherent in accepting handouts, and it was relatively easy for John to overcome the natural timidity of the hungry quail. They, like chickens, would come to feed when called and became so gentle that when he squatted down some of them would hop up on his arm and eat grain or bread crumbs out of his hand.

When Haley Aycock, John's nephew, was out of school

one summer, he tamed a coyote pup and a ground squirrel. According to stories that have weathered the passage of time, the squirrel would scamper back and forth across Haley's shoulders until another person approached. Then the cautious squirrel would dive into Haley's shirt pocket, turn around and ease his head out of the opening. If the way was clear he would resume his perch on the shoulder, but if danger seemed imminent he would duck back down and stay there until he deemed sufficient time had elapsed for him to stick his head out again and reconnoiter. This playful pet was the clown of the camp and much appreciated by everyone.

Evetts has mentioned in recent years that he once mounted a redheaded woodpecker, and for this taxidermic effort was paid the supreme compliment. One day at the ranch, while everyone was away, a chaparral got in the shack. Apparently deceived by the realistic workmanship and believing the woodpecker to be alive, he jumped on the stuffed bird and tore it to pieces. It is not easy to fool a roadrunner.

Our land is often bleak and uninspiring, but it can be utterly charming. A cowboy sometimes consciously breathes in the heavenly aroma of wet greasewood after a shower, and about dusk he marvels at bullbats feeding in the air. He might laugh with glee as one of them dives at a pebble he flips toward the sky. And this lover of solitude, in the cool darkness of early evening, basks in glowing contentment as he enjoys the choral effect of his horse munching grain, accompanied by the soft soothing notes of a slowly turning windmill. Then the cowboy can lie on his bedroll in the dark of the moon and see a million stars. Occasional meteor showers induce wonder and childlike anticipation. Nobody lives better than this, and he is confident, perhaps even smug, in his conviction that he is one of God's chosen. John was happy to be back in such an environment.

Though the cowboy might have no religious persuasion,

he tends to believe that God is always involved in the cow business. In fact, no thoughtful person raised in the country believes that Mother Nature (perceived by many to be one of God's manifestations) is indifferent. Rather she is like strict, intelligent mothers the world over who are much more solicitous of the child's future than of its immediate affection. Although Mother Nature is ever mindful of the soul-soothing value of beauty, tenderness, and temporary respite from stress, she nevertheless conditions her children for tomorrow's harsh realities by imposing immediate and painful penalties for any violation of her imperatives. The ones who are unwilling or unable to comply with her admonitions suffer grievously. They are banished to town.

One of the first lessons learned by the early settlers in the Pecos Valley area was that the powers-that-be in Austin had not been communing with Nature. The four sections allotted to each family under the latest homestead act were woefully inadequate. Topsoil in this particular area is much too thin to grow crops. The underground water supply is deep, insufficient, and, in fairly extensive blocks of land, nonexistent. The rainfall, as has already been mentioned, is uncertain to say the least. Eventually it was learned that a family needs a minimum of sixteen sections to eke out a living year in and year out. Some managed to scrimp by on less, but theirs could properly be called bare subsistence. Most homesteaders soon realized that the only hope for economic survival was to buy more land.

A few wily old cowmen, knowledgeable about the possibilities and limitations of the country, bought larger tracts and waited for the inevitable. When the disillusioned homesteaders had to fold up, one or the other of the ranchers bought the place or simply ran his cattle on it until the state made some other dispensation.

The frugal, stubborn owners of some of the smaller places

held on for years, their holdings popularly and accurately referred to as starve-outs. On one of the worst starve-outs in the area, six or seven miles east of John's camp, lived one of his neighbors—a much older man named Wood Birdwell. Mr. Birdwell supplemented his meager income by doing day-work for nearby ranchers, and often he and John simply swapped work. For some years he was the one John depended on when help was needed. One such time was when John's Model-T broke down and the problem was something he couldn't handle by himself. After supper he saddled up and started over to Mr. Birdwell's place.

"I knew it was going to be awful dark that night," John said, "so while I could still see a little I took my bearings and judged that if I could keep the wind quartering in to my face just right I could make it across there." What he had not counted on was a gentle shift in the wind direction. "I trotted along for about an hour and pulled up. I couldn't see anything. I knew about where I should be, but nothing felt right. Damn, it was dark. I sat there on my horse for a while and decided to go back home and wait for morning." Fortunately for cowboys who refuse to sleep at night, a horse can always find his way back home.

John went on with his story. "Early next morning I started again. About halfway there I topped a little hill and saw a rider come over a rise about a mile in front of me. I could tell by the way he sat his horse and by the fact that he never moved his head that it was old Wood. I often wondered since he never looked left or right how he ever saw any cattle, but he did. He saw everything. We rode up side by side facing opposite directions, and he still hadn't turned his head toward me. 'Good morning, Wood. I was just going over to your place to see if you could help me fix my car.'

'Morning. I was just heading to your place for the same thing. Where is your car?'

'It's at the house. Where is yours?'

'About halfway between here and Pyote. Let's fix yours first so we can use it to go get mine. Otherwise we will have to carry our tools and parts horseback or use a wagon.'

"I was agreeable to that plan," John said as his story wound down, "so I turned my horse around, and we headed to the ranch. He still hadn't turned his head toward me."

Mechanical breakdowns notwithstanding, they found time that year to load the shack on a wagon bed and move it to what is now called the Old Place. John and Evetts had built some working corrals there and since Papa had added five sections to the north side this was a more central location for the camp.

They did not move the garage. Earlier John had scrounged enough old lumber to build a garage for Henry Ford's epitome of mechanical caprice, and after he and Wood Birdwell put the finishing touches on this flimsy structure late one afternoon, they decided to let Mr. Birdwell's car be the first to sleep inside. "Drive her in, Wood," John invited, "and let's see how she fits."

"Hell, I'm not going to drive that thing into that little old place. You do it."

John, always ready for anything, jumped into Wood's Model-T and drove it in—through the back of the garage and out again. He had to give it so much gas to get up the ramp that he was unable to stop before he ran out of room. The planning must have been faulty. Maybe the ramp should have been fifty feet longer. In any event it was never rebuilt.

Shortage of water has plagued cowmen over much of West Texas for generations, and that is the condition that greeted John on his return to the ranch. There were no wells on the five sections Papa bought in 1917, therefore there was grass for more cattle than he could water—an intolerable situation from John's point of view. He decided that two more wells

44

were needed; an additional well at the Old Place and a well three miles northwest of there, near the center of the Pimm country.

John acquired from Will Brookfield an old skeleton of a water-well machine which, having been parked out in the pasture for years, bore all the ravages of time and neglect. He and Evetts somehow got it loaded on the running gear of a wagon and took it to the Pimm location. They patched the thing up and for power used an old five-horse gasoline engine, mounted on a frame with iron wheels and a wagon tongue. When the rig was operable, the men moved their chuck-box and bedrolls to the drilling site and began the slow, arduous task of drilling a well with primitive equipment.

Drilling technology has improved considerably since the early twenties. Nowadays a modern rotary machine, using air, can drill a well two hundred feet deep in a matter of hours. Back then a cable tool rig with small light tools might make from four to ten feet in hard formations in a twelve-hour day. Nobody remembers exactly how long it took to drill this well, but apparently there was time enough to complete the well and for John, Evetts, and Wood Birdwell to pour a concrete bottom in the steel tank before Evetts went back to college. Pouring concrete was not so fast and easy then, for most ranchers hauled sand from the nearest wash, mixed the cement with hoes and shovels, scooped it out of the mixing trough into buckets and handed the buckets over the side of the tank to the man inside. Strands of old barbed wire, too rotten to put back in a fence, were twisted together and used for reinforcement. The same method was employed for pouring the concrete water troughs. There was one leak in the concrete at the Pimm which was patched the following year, and though the tank was in use for over sixty years before it was replaced, it never again leaked through the bottom.

An interesting aside to this project is perhaps permissible.

Evetts went back to school, little suspecting that the ground-work for part of his fame was laid in the scanty shade of an old water-well drilling machine. Not for his unique skill with a pen, nor his sound and steadfast political views, but for his artistry with yeast and flour. The summer of 1922 was when Evetts—taking full advantage of Wood Birdwell's expertise—learned to make sourdough biscuits. The biscuits, unlike his political opinions, never failed to win wholehearted approval.

John could not have forseen this kindness of fate, for he was much too busy making preparations for drilling the next well. He elected to set up an engine at the Pimm to pump water for the near term, and put up a windmill when he had more time. Another hand was hired; the rig was moved to the Old Place and John could once again enjoy the luxury of sleeping inside.

By late fall he was ready to begin and believed that since the screwworm season was over and the cattle were shaped up for winter, they could drill twenty-four hours a day. The only drawback to this plan was the engine at the Pimm place. Keeping that engine going would take up a sizable portion of one man's time, even if he never got left afoot. Usually, the hand—unfortunately Daddy could not remember his name when he told this story—ran the engine and looked after the cattle that watered there. He always carried oil and gasoline horseback, so this was never a thirty-minute job. While the hand tended to the engine and the cattle at the Pimm, John himself kept drilling at the Old Place. When he noticed something wrong with a cow or calf he would shut down and take care of the cattle. He and his hand spelled each other during the night, but neither got much sleep. John used to tell that one morning about three o'clock the hand came into the shack and said: "Wake up, John. I just lost the tools in the hole, ha ha ha!"

"I don't see anything so damn funny about that," was the

grumpy retort. And as a matter of fact, John didn't seem to find anything funny about it forty years later.

"I got up," he said, "and we got the forge going and made a fishing tool, got the tools out of the hole and were back to drilling by daylight."

Evetts tells a story indicative of John's lack of rest and his preoccupation with the job at hand. "I was home for Christmas and drilling that night when I needed something from the shack," Evetts recalled. "I took the coal-oil lantern and stepped into the shack. There was John, sitting up in his bedroll and apparently searching for something with his right hand. He was grasping here, there, and everywhere and was obviously agitated. 'What are you looking for?' I asked.

"'The line—I can't find the line. I think there's some slack in it. We have to keep the slack out of the line.'

"'John—I'm drilling, and there is no slack in the line. Now go back to sleep.' He slid back down in his bed and went back to sleep," Evetts recalled with a grin, "if he was ever awake."

≈

Let us, for a little while, leave John with his nightmare of a slack drilling line causing the dreaded crooked hole, and meet the Brookfields.

The Brookfield brothers started buying land in this area about 1909 and owned separate but adjoining ranches. The purchase Papa made in 1917, known as the Pimm place, was originally acquired from the state in 1905 by a lady of that name and is sandwiched between the Schumm place and the Brookfield holdings. The W. W. (Will) Brookfield ranch was on the north side of the Pimm place and the house was about five miles due north of where John was wrestling—even in his sleep—with the problems of drilling a water well.

Will Brookfield was a tall spare man with a penchant for fast cars and buried treasure. Stories of his futile search for gold and his inability to cope with the marvels of the bur-

47

geoning automotive industry must have been repeated end-lessly, for they are the only ones that live in my fading memory. Nevertheless, he was always confident and eager to embark on his next "can't miss" scheme for finding untold riches, even as he sported a neck brace from the latest mishap with his beloved Buick.

Mrs. Brookfield was another matter. She was a woman of awesome proportions who always wore what appeared to a child to be the same long bluish dress and seldom left the ranch. She was a comfortable lady for children to be around, until she saw a mouse; she was unafraid of anything else on earth, but a mouse always got her attention. When I was about four years old, Mrs. Brookfield, Mama, and Mama Haley were fixing dinner at our house. My brother Gene and I were outside in the yard when I heard my first "inhuman scream." (After some thought, I don't believe I have heard anything like it since.) My hair hadn't quite settled down before I heard Mama Haley exclaim:

"Mrs. Brookfield! What on earth is the matter with you?"

"I saw a mouse."

"Mrs. Brookfield, a mouse is nothing to be afraid of. Now get down off that chair before. . . ."

That was all I heard, for it seemed to me that distance was most desirable, and I was earnestly attending this need. It was probably a good thing Daddy was working cattle as it is unlikely that his uncontrollable laughter would have set very well with a large, vigorous woman frightened half out of her wits.

There was one other memorable incident involving Mrs. Brookfield. At least Mama's periodic complaining the next few years made it memorable. Daddy made fairly frequent

48

stops at the Brookfield place, probably because they were getting on in years and might be in need. This time the whole family was along, and as we were getting into the Model-T to start home, Mrs. Brookfield rushed out of the house waving her arms. She talked with a southern accent and as she came up to Daddy's side of the car she drawled:

"John, I almost forgot. I want you to grease that windmill before you leave. That old towuh's so rickety that I'm afraid for Wilbuh to climb up on it. It might fall down with him."

Daddy laughed, struck a trot to the mill, and Mama did a slow burn. From time to time for several years Mama would tell someone of Mrs. Brookfield's request and always end the story by saying:

"It was perfectly alright for that old tower to collapse when my husband was on it, but she wasn't going to let her husband take any chances."

Cornering in to the Will Brookfield place was a small ranch owned by his brother Victor. Old Vic, as John referred to him, and his wife lived west of Will's place. About eight miles of grass and brush lay between the houses and a million miles of nothing between the personalities. The only link was real estate. My own lingering impression of the Victor Brookfields is that he was a dour, taciturn man and she was a flibbertigibbet with shrewish tendencies. When asked about this years later, Daddy did not quarrel with my memory of Mrs. Brookfield, but told me I was dead wrong about Vic.

"Old Vic hardly ever laughed out loud, but he did have a good, dry sense of humor. He was a hard worker and knew how to do lots of things. He was a well-driller and had his own rig. He was a pretty good carpenter, a pretty good hand horseback, and a hell of a country blacksmith. He was the best welder with a forge I ever saw."

Daddy was seldom lavish with praise, but his endorsement of Victor Brookfield was generous indeed.

VI

John always carried a pocket notebook and one of those handy little encased pencils that feed companies used to pass out as advertisements. Most cowboys carried something like that to keep a running record of the cattle count, but John had a peculiar habit of jotting down unrelated reminders or observations. Several of these notebooks, plus other written memos, are in my possession and have enabled me to be uncharacteristically precise with dates.

For some reason which she can no longer remember, my mother transcribed some of his random notes onto five pages of what looks like Big Chief tablet paper. The first entry is dated 1905 and reads: "Miles, Tex. First year in school." The last date mentioned is 1933. It would have been nice to let these biographical notes take the place of the first chapters of this account, but they are just too brief. For example:

1923

"Bought 150 head of yearling heifers @ $30, 100 head of cows and calves @ $45. Entire amt. $9,000. In the fall of 1923 bought 111 head of calves for $2997."

1924

"In May 1924, we sold our 1923 calf crop @ $31 per head. On Dec. 1st I married."

"Bought 6 bulls for $360. Sold our 1924 calf crop in spring of 1925 for $4000. Sold 1925 calf crop for $6000.

That wraps up a three-year span of his life and most of the important points were covered. He told us the number and classes of cattle purchased and the price paid. He left us, however, guessing about the number of calves in the calf crops sold, and also the details of his courtship and marriage were a bit sketchy. We still do not know anything about the courtship, but we can furnish the name of the bride.

Florence May Trent was born March 21, 1907, in Monahans, Texas, the only daughter of Henry Arthur (Bud) and Elizabeth Trent. Bud was a carpenter by trade, and the family was living in Pyote when John left his job in the oil field and moved back to the ranch. Bud had worked on ranches a good part of his life, and Florence had spent more time in the country than in town.

Many of her childhood memories relate to incidents or experiences on ranches, and, like others of that era, one of her most vivid is the 1918 blizzard. Though she was going to school at the time and staying in town with her mother, her daddy was working on a ranch west of Odessa and was on his way to town when the storm hit the area. Bud and a friend left the sandhills ranch west of the Caprock that morning in an "open" wagon. According to Florence, Bud's companion was of Italian descent and had legally changed his name to Joe White. (The story goes that White's playful friends accused him of doing so only because he couldn't pronounce the old family name.) The storm overtook them on the stark plains east of the sands, and the two cowboys with a tiring team were in for a struggle. It is more than likely—and perhaps ironic— that national origin and cowboy humor were frozen in limbo that frigid afternoon and the warmth of amiable repartee was denied the two old friends as they fought their way crosswind through a raging blizzard to the safety of Odessa. They must have made it just in time, for Florence recalls that neither man was in good condition, but Mr. White was very close to the end of his endurance.

When John and Florence met she was living with her parents in Pyote and working for Jack Sitton in his combination general store and post office. Florence was fond of her boss, but she delights in revealing that he was a little hard on the thin pine flooring supported by floor joists set too far apart. The damage usually occurred when Sitton decided to rearrange the stock. A big, powerful man with a hundred pound sack of flour on one shoulder and another under an arm was just too much weight on too little displacement. Every now and then an overloaded board broke under Jack's heavy tread. When this happened, Florence relates with a chuckle: "Jack would just place an empty nail keg over the hole in the floor." Apparently, he never replaced a broken board, and his customers, well aware of Jack's nonchalant attitude towards maintenance, cheerfully and with appropriate comments threaded their way through the challenging maze of nail kegs. But fate, or Cupid, was about to take a hand and Florence was not to enjoy this pleasant, carefree living much longer.

A whirlwind in the form of John Furman Haley was approaching, bent on shattering the serenity of the elder Trents and disrupting the smooth operation of Jack Sitton's general store. On December 1, 1924, Florence and John were married in the Baptist church at Pecos, Texas, and a high lope would be her gait for the next thirty years.

After the ceremony they drove to the ranch in John's old Studebaker touring car, from which the top had long since been removed. Lack of money and extra help forbade the traditional honeymoon. Someone had to look after the livestock.

John learned right away that the quarters for a man and a happy bride must be considerably larger than those required for two men. L. W. Anderson, a man of some means and vastly more experienced in the whims of women and the ways of the world, came to the aid of his frustrated friend and pupil. He had a small two-room dilapidated structure a few miles from the Old Place that was no longer in use, and he told John he could have it. So once again the team was hitched to a jury-rigged wagon, and John pulled out to bring this bounty home and attach it to his own ten-by-fourteen shack. Mr. Anderson's generosity combined with quite a lot of John's sweat served to swell Florence's living area to a spacious 476 square feet. But before Florence could find enough cast-off furniture to fill this luxurious area, they moved.

Papa Haley bought the Brawley Oates ranch, located in Winkler County about seven miles northeast of the Old Place, in March 1926. John was told to move—forthwith. Though he probably regretted the abandonment of his most ambitious construction effort since building the garage, the move itself could not have been much of a chore. John and Florence could have put everything they owned in about the same amount of space taken up by Florence's clothes when they moved—for the last time—about forty years later.

The Oates place was an old "W" watering—Johnson Brothers founded a 1200 section ranch in the mid 1880s and branded the W. They built good double-strand barbed wire corrals at every watering, dug a big dirt tank, and fed it with two windmills. Their system was so distinctive that to this day it is possible to recognize some of the "W" waterings by the remains of a tank or segments of an old corral.

There was a rather rambling house with high ceilings and shiplap siding, with an open porch on the south side. It was on a little rise about 100 yards south of the remaining windmill—the other had been taken down—and looked over the barn and corrals. Mama appreciated the spaciousness but complained that in the wintertime what warmth the old house managed to contain always hovered about six feet above floor level.

An old place by 1926 standards, and badly run down, the ranch was made to order for a man with endless energy and a driving work ethic. One man in one lifetime could not possibly do everything that needed to be done. Most men would have been dismayed and intimidated by such a prospect; John was ecstatic.

He saw right away that far too much water from the huge dirt tank was being lost through seepage and evaporation; he wasted little time in doing something about it. In 1927, with team and fresno, he built a smaller tank on the south side of the mill, using the dirt from one side of the existing tank.

Moving dirt with a fresno and team is slow, boring work and no comic relief can be expected, but throughout his lifetime John seemed to serve as a catalyst for unlikely humor. As the new tank was slowly taking shape, Bill Dublin, who lived just over the line in New Mexico, stopped by to deliver a letter.

"I saw Bill drive up about the time I loaded my fresno, and by the time I dumped it he was standin' there with a letter in his hand. He handed it to me and took the lines all in the same motion. The team never stopped moving, and I opened the letter as Bill started after another load. I was still readin' when he got back with the next load of dirt. Bill had lost one hand just above the wrist, and I started watching to see how in the hell he was going to handle the lines and dump that fresno with one hand. I hadn't noticed, and I don't think Bill knew about it, but the seam in his britches had ripped out and he must not have been wearing any shorts, for when he pulled past me and squatted to catch the fresno handle, everything —just sort of fell out. I got tickled, and Bill started another round. The same thing happened again, and I kept laughing. 'That must be a damned funny letter,' Bill said. I told him it sure was, thanked him for takin' the trouble and took the lines back. About thirty minutes later it dawned on me that I never did see how he handled that job with just one hand."

John and Florence settled into a familiar routine, or as close to it as John could come. The Oates place was to be their home for the next thirty years, and the ranch as a whole, John's primary interest in life. They raised two boys—John Arthur, born August 1926, and Robert Eugene, born October 1928—rebuilt the old house in 1932, and generally improved the ranch. It was the usual grind from there—working long hours, trying to pay the bills on time, saving money if they ever got any, and worrying about their always stubborn and sometimes violent children. They struggled and coped, much the same way as all young parents. Except John was not a slave to the tyranny of habit. Systematic procedure played no part in his philosophical approach to any task or problem. There was always something unexpected, a crisis, or a series of crises. The very nature of the cow business renders it vulnerable to the unexpected, but when Daddy was around there seemed to be something more. It must have been ordained that he would forever thwart habitual regularity. The only habit anyone might have developed within John's sphere was starting the workday (which was every day) long before dawn and finishing after dark. That routine suited him right down to the ground, but it never caught on with the general public.

On November 1, 1930, Papa Haley bought six sections from Will P. Edwards. That land was not the best tract in this range, but it was the connecting link for his scattered holdings. With the acquisition of the Oates and Edwards country, John now had an additional thirty-five or forty miles of fence to keep in repair, several windmills to maintain, and more cattle to look after. He needed three or four full-time hands.

He usually had one. That might explain, in part, why there were so many crises. Lest we give the wrong impression: the cattle always had water, the fences were kept up, and the livestock received proper care, which says quite a lot about the hours John worked and his organizational ability.

VII

About the time John moved to the Oates place, oil was discovered near the present town of Wink, and the county population zoomed from some eighty people to estimates as high as 40,000 at the height of the boom. This was not the first oil strike in the Permian Basin area, but it was the first in Winkler County. From the beginning, the production of oil replaced agriculture as the economic mainstay, thereby changing forever the way of life of area ranchers.

It might be in order to discuss oil booms in general for just a bit. When a disproportionate number of people flock into any area, they face a lot of obstacles, most of them logistical. Water, gas, roads, sewerage, electric power, schools and police departments must be found, installed, built, organized and financed. Usually, municipal bonds are sold and a "temporary" increase in the ad valorem tax is levied to defray the initial cost and provide maintenance for the projects. All too often the boom fizzles. (In 1936, ten years after the discovery of oil near Wink, another "discovery" in the north end of the county precipitated a short-lived boom in Kermit.) The city, county and schools are sometimes managed by glib but inept administrators who, through their persuasiveness, manage to saddle the residents with a monstrous debt that must be serviced. Added to that expense is the upkeep of unneeded municipal buildings and the payment for services that are no longer essential. As the search for and production of oil decline, an exodus begins, and the ad valorem taxpayer is left to finance the excesses imposed upon him by voting drifters who pay no local taxes. Ranchers consider this circumstance a far greater threat to their livelihoods than depressions and drouths. These risks are inherent, expected, and in most cases finally resolved successfully—at great and often unjustifiable expense. Troubles of this nature leave no enduring impression, except on the ones who pay the bills.

Conversely, the people who follow booms incite great interest and provoke unlimited and undying stories. When it came to color, the boomers were matchless. The escapades of these unique people fascinate the general public, and they also catch the attention of anthropologists and sociologists. As if by magic, people hundreds of miles away know within hours when a wildcat well in a large unexplored area "blows out." The influx begins immediately. They all come, the avid storekeepers and saloon keepers, those innovative providers for other people's needs, the hardworking, hard-drinking roughnecks and roustabouts, many of them with flexible consciences, the sober family men looking for a better way to feed and clothe their children, and all the other people it takes to run an oil field and form a community. Most of them realize, and some even admit, in their declining years, that it was not the prospect of riches but the thrill of the quest that drove them from boom to boom.

The boomtowns of the 1920s suffered through or enjoyed, depending on the point of view, a circumstance not present after "repeal." The country during that era was writhing under the yoke of the "noble experiment," which was the first effort by meddlesome do-gooders to legislate a perfect society. Yet a small core of hardened men who had nothing but contempt for any law—whether God's or manmade—infested every community. These men, through intimidation, bribery and coercion furnished the commodities that appeal to man's baser appetites, and they seemed to thrive in new towns with inadequate law enforcement. The prohibition amendment not only created a ready-made multibillion dollar business for moonshiners and bootleggers, but it also placed outside the pale of legality every person in the United States who enjoyed a drink. A large majority of the people in boomtowns did enjoy their booze—hard-shelled Baptists were always a minority—and the drinkers, along with the bootleggers, thought of every conceivable way to circumvent this unpopular law. Consequently the children who grew up under these conditions had a tendency to pick and choose the laws they thought should be obeyed and to consider it their patriotic duty to flout the others.

John Haley was no stranger to boomtowns, but heretofore he had been one of the hands, one of the merrymakers. During the Wink boom he was forced into an unfamiliar role. He became, or so it seemed to his children, a permanent member of the Winkler County grand jury. All adults know that those jurors are replaced every six months, but nobody could have convinced me at the time.

I have not attempted to research the matter, but at least one grand jury panel must have been returning significant indictments, for the beating of individual members became a favorite pastime of the local thugs. As an object lesson, they once severely mauled an unfortunate juror, tied him to the back of a car, and dragged him down the main street of Wink. This vengeance failed in its purpose because most of those doughty supporters of law and order could not be intimidated. Daddy told me years later: "I made up my mind at the start that those bastards might kill me, but they sure as hell weren't going to beat me to death. I carried a gun everywhere I went."

John had a gun in each hand the night two carloads of punks attempted to "box" him on his way to the ranch. My mother, who was with him, recalled: "Those guys must have decided that the show wouldn't be worth the price of admission, for they backed off that night and never made another serious threat." Such were the hazards of "true bills."

Those were exciting times, but the 1929 market crash had already changed the focus of the world. Even the activity of boomtowns became subdued during a world-wide depression. There have been irregular periods of "boom and bust" throughout the history of our country, but the results were never so dreadful. As the Great Depression wore on and on, it seemed to destroy the people's confidence that they could govern themselves and look after their own welfare. The majority of the people in Winkler County were no exception. Frantic activity engendered by the oil strike was already ebbing, and the sturdy boomers, like everyone else, were caught in an economic squeeze. For the first time the nation's voters placed personal freedom at the bottom of their list of priorities. They wanted a keeper. They got one.

Franklin D. Roosevelt took office in 1933, and a drouth in West Texas began the same year. The western prairies eventually received the needed moisture, but the political drouth continues unabated. Before the rains came, however, John Haley and everyone else in the cow business endured some miserable times. The economic destruction from the Wall Street avalanche was almost complete. Certainly, the cattle industry found no shelter. Fort Worth was still the nearest market for canner and cutter cattle, and, reminiscent of 1918, the ranchers were reluctant to ship their livestock to market when there was considerable doubt as to whether the freight bill could be recovered. The situation is familiar. The ever-optimistic ranchers hoped the Depression would be short-lived and surely, surely it would "rain in time." Neither event occurred, and the cowmen went into the winter of 1933 and 1934 with growing herds—but their optimism had begun to fade.

When Mother Nature decides to clobber man with a drouth, she needs no help. Nevertheless, coincidence and governmental forces joined the cloudless skies to form a triumvirate that seemed almost malevolent in its assault on western ranchers.

The most unlovable characteristic of a successful politician is that as soon as the votes are counted he deems himself eminently qualified to manage other people's affairs. The new administration, early in 1933, wasted no time in formulating and instituting a huge and classically socialistic system of bureaus with frightening powers. According to my uncle, J. Evetts Haley, who wrote an article that appeared in the December 8, 1934, edition of the *Saturday Evening Post*, the farmers and ranchers were probably most affected by the Agricultural Adjustment Administration (AAA) and the Agricultural Credit Corporation (ACC). That article is the source of much of the following information.

In an effort to control over-production and thus strengthen prices, the bureaucrats in 1933 imposed a restriction on the number of acres that could be sown in cotton and corn— the two commodities that cowmen need since the cattle in the country were kept alive on cottonseed cake and fattened in the feedlots on corn. They further reduced the allowable acreage in 1934. At the same time the Agricultural Credit Corporation, the illegitimate competitor of bona fide bankers, made thousands of injudicious loans, thereby postponing the liquidation of hundreds of herds.

Now for the coincidence: while the government was severely curtailing the number of acres on which crops could be planted, the major and widespread drouth seriously restricted the yield of those limited acres. The resulting shortage of cottonseed sent the price of cottonseed cake soaring to forty dollars a ton as the price of calves slipped under ten dollars a head. The price of corn made it impossible to feed tendollar calves and show a profit. All those factors served to create an enormous buildup of cattle numbers, and the ranchers, unable to afford the artificially inflated cost of feed, could only watch helplessly as their cattle began to die.

In 1933, the AAA and its subdivisions implemented a drouth-relief program. Certain counties within certain states were declared eligible to sell their cattle to the federal government. The AAA would pay twelve dollars per head for cows and four dollars for calves, which was twice as much as legitimate packers could afford. The option rested with the cowmen—they could sell or not, as they chose. Nearly all of them chose to participate in the program, and they gathered the cattle they wished to sell and held them for inspection by a government agent. The agent in turn looked over the herd and culled the cattle that were too weak to make the trip to one of the many processing plants. The "condemned" culls were shot and left to rot in the pasture. The rest were trailed to the nearest shipping point. The owner, or rather the recent owner, could butcher any of the "condemned" cattle that he thought were edible. Naturally he could not sell any of the meat, but what really griped his western soul was that it was against the law to give it away.

Under this program the government bought nearly seven million head of cattle. About one million of this number were "condemned" and killed on the range. The program did indeed bail thousands of cowmen out of an awful mess but at fearful cost to the American taxpayer.

I cannot verify the number of cattle the Haleys delivered to the government in October 1934, but there is one number which I shall never forget. Daddy and his crew butchered twenty-one of the condemned vealer calves one evening after dark. My bedtime was excused, and I was allowed to help. That was one of those experiences which stick in a child's memory. Recently, in answer to a probing question about this matter, my mother, with a touch of regret and anger in her voice, replied. "I don't remember, John. I never wanted to remember. The only thing I can tell you is the meat from those little old dogied calves was horrible." We had no refrigeration at the ranch in those days, so the carcasses were hung in the Wink icehouse, and some of them were promptly stolen. That incident marks the only time within my memory when neither Daddy nor Mama seemed particularly exercised by a thief's depredation.

Papa Haley had formed a partnership with Daddy and Evetts prior to this time, and the Haley group, as already mentioned, elected to sell some of their cattle. On delivering cattle and before receiving payment they were forced to sign something called the Emergency Cattle Agreement which all but consigned their collective soul as well as their business to the disposition of the Department of Agriculture. To my knowledge no Haley has joined a government program since.

The fall of 1934 and still no rain: John would be hard-pressed to "winter" what cattle were left. He conceived the idea of grinding what is called bear grass in West Texas— soapweed in Arizona, and I don't know what all in other parts of the country—and using it as a substitute for cottonseed cake. This plant resembles a yucca: the leaves or spines are very narrow, taper gradually to a sharp point, and are extremely tough. The trunk or stem to which the spines are attached is from three to six inches in diameter and fairly short, at least in this area. The stem is usually completely hidden by dead spines that have fallen outward and down. Daddy bought an old feed-grinder that had a shallow trough with conveyor chains in the bottom, extending perhaps six or eight feet back from the rollers and knives. He powered this contraption with a drive-belt looped over a drum attached to the jacked-up rear wheel of a Model-T Ford. The little mill was designed to chop grain sorghum and was much too light for the tough bear grass, but it didn't cost much and Daddy was a pretty good "fix-it" hand. There were innumerable breakdowns, but the cattle were fed.

John hired a cook and tried to keep a crew of five or six men. They camped as near as possible to where the bear grass was plentiful, took the chuck box out of the wagon, set it on a stand, and used the wagon to bring the bear grass to the grinder. One man went in front and burned the dead spines. Two men followed, one of whom cut the stem with an axe; then the other threw the bear grass on the wagon, which a fourth man was driving. When the wagon was filled, it was driven back to the grinder where two more men were chopping up the previous wagonload. That is, this was the routine if everything was functioning properly. When the chopped feed got too deep in front of the grinder, it was shoveled by hand into piles on either side. Later it was shoveled onto the wagon, taken to the feed grounds, and shoveled into the troughs. Just enough high-priced cottonseed meal was sprinkled on the roughage to make it palatable.

The cattle did not fatten on this ration, but they did make it through the winter. For that matter they seemed to winter better than the men. The hours were long and grueling and the turnover in men was fierce. Only one man stayed with John all winter. Millions of people were looking for work, but not that kind of work, and John was often shorthanded. Fifteen years later, in another drouth, someone asked Daddy in my presence if he would consider feeding bear grass again. "No," he replied, "it was too rough." I knew right then that feeding bear grass would never be one of my alternatives, although it did keep J. A. Haley & Sons in the cow business

until it began to rain a little in 1935.

The early thirties were lean times but not devoid of humor, as one of the oft-repeated stories of a horse trade will attest. Daddy traded a two-year-old colt for a milk cow and fifteen turkeys to Jess Hensley, who lived about seven miles southeast of Wink. They traded sight unseen, and Daddy was to make the switch. He left the ranch horseback early one morning, led the colt to Hensley's place, put him in a corral, found the cow, and started back home. On the way back, John was driving the cow down the west side of Wink when just in front of them a woman started walking across the road, and here we will leave the story to Daddy:

"I traded the colt to Jess because the horse was mean. Well, hell, I didn't have any idea that his Jersey cow might be meaner'n my horse. When that lady stepped out into the street I thought the cow would booger and try to come back by me, but she wasn't any ordinary cow. She just looked at the lady a minute, then charged and ran right over the top of her. Well I was mad and embarrassed, so I roped that damn cow and tied her to a bush, then went back and apologized to the lady. Even the apology didn't seem to help her feelings much, so I was still mad at the cow when I went back to turn her loose. And before I could get that done, I'll be damned if she didn't run over me. I was beginning to have doubts about that trade."

There were a lot of things that cow didn't like, including smart-aleck kids, and she was destined to earn the kind of reputation that is usually reserved for mean pitching horses. I don't know how Daddy got the turkeys home, but everybody remembers that the local coyotes were sure glad to see them.

VIII

The condition of the cattle and the range gradually improved through 1935, but even so a lot of people, including Daddy, were hard-pressed to meet their obligations and put beans on the table. His kids were in school, and they had to be boarded out in town. Expenses were piling up and John reasoned that extra expense called for extra effort. Since he had some free time at night, he decided to try something new —again. (He had been a candidate for the sheriff's office in a recent election and the revelation that he was not a politician came as no particular surprise.)

That summer, he built an open-air dance platform at the ranch and hired a band for Saturday nights. Potential customers faced a drive of about fifteen miles over a rough country road with a couple of gates along the way, but they came to the dances. Nothing intimidates hunters and party-goers.

The Wink boom had run its course by 1935 and the drifters had moved to new pastures, but the people who remained were a spirited bunch who must have been born with a craving for action. Some of John's friends advised against the dance-floor project. They cautioned that most of his customers would be rowdy holdovers from the dying boomtown, and that he could expect little or no help from law enforcement officers because he lived too far from town. John believed, however, that if the people enjoyed the outing, they would not want to jeopardize the source of enjoyment. He also felt that his friends were dependable; they could be counted on for solid support should any group become troublesome.

One episode might have furnished some credence for the doubters' misgivings, but it definitely supplied credibility for John's faith in his friends. A contentious fellow got out of hand, and John worked him over with a piece of chain. "That guy has a bunch of in-laws living in Wink," his friends exclaimed. "They are a tough bunch, all knife-men, and they will be out here next week to cut you down." As a youngster, I had heard only bits and pieces of this story, and in response to my request for details some years later, Daddy replied:

"Well, I didn't think too much about it to start with, for I knew most of those people, and I didn't think they liked that bastard any more than I did. But sure enough, when the next Saturday rolled around they all showed up. They weren't drinking much and seemed to be having a good time, but I kept a close eye on them just the same. They were tough and a little mean, and I didn't want to get 'sandwiched.' I was icing down some soft drinks when a big burly friend of mine walked up—wearing a jacket. We shook hands, and with his other hand he pulled back one side of his jacket so I could see the .45 automatic in his belt. 'Watch 'em, John,' he said, 'but don't worry. If they start anything, I'll kill every son of a bitch and throw you the gun. They'll never stick you for it.' I sure was glad those guys didn't do anything, for ol' Bill would have done just what he said he would do." Nobody ever knew whether Bill's stated intention was overheard, or the danger just sensed. In either case the evening was uneventful, which argued that ol' Bill's awesome presence tended to bring out the best in folks.

Daddy must have been making a little money, for when the novelty of dancing in the open became chilled by the crisp fall nights, he doubled the floor space and closed it in. Coleman lanterns furnished adequate light, and big coal-burning heaters, which adapted nicely to wood, kept the place warm and snug as he started having dances twice a week. This routine lasted through the winter. Then John moved the building to Kermit. Oil had been discovered just north of town.

John chose a location out on the west side. The building faced south and was located on the north side of the old Wink highway about a block east of the railroad. He named this establishment Tascosa. The family's living quarters were attached to the back; that is, two small rooms separated by a passageway were added. Daddy and Mama occupied one of the rooms and my brother Gene and I slept in the other. The hall was the well-traveled route from the bar and dance floor to the outhouse and cowshed. Of course, the beer-drinking patrons were not much interested in the cowshed, unless the outhouse was occupied.

The cowshed and its occupant might be a little out of place in most towns today, even illegal in some progressive communities. But no comment was elicited in those practical times, for people were much too busy trying to scratch out a living. They had neither the time nor the inclination to propose laws designed to regulate the habits or idiosyncrasies of their neighbors. Besides, the chore of milking a cow twice a day helps keep kids out of trouble.

The building itself fit right in with boomtown decor. It was a simple frame structure, squatting under a sheet iron roof, with its flanks protected by sheet iron siding. There was a trucking company just east of the Tascosa and a mud company to the west; the rest of the immediate area was residential, at least early in the boom. Hundreds of tents appeared to have

71

sprung from the sandy soil amidst the mesquite and catclaw with no sense of design or symmetry. The ubiquitous outhouse —that standardized fixture of necessity—stood directly behind each tent like a uniformed sentinel, dutifully fulfilling its purpose but adding nothing that was pleasing to the eye.

As might be expected, aesthetics were not one of John's primary concerns; what troubled him was the limited number of hours in a day. The demands of the honky-tonk (which, in 1936, was the popular name in the "oil patch" for any place of business that sold beer and held dances) were taking a lot of his time; many more hours were "wasted" in the pickup, as he drove back and forth between Kermit and the ranch. A more direct way would be opened shortly, but until then the route still passed through Wink. John found it increasingly difficult to furnish the necessary help for his only steady hand, a young man named Gene Forsythe. And Gene had his hands full, for soaking rains had fallen that year, the country was blooming, and the livestock were vulnerable to the flesh-eating screwworm.

This parasite is the vermiform larva stage of the prolific blowfly, which regards every open sore as an inviting incubator. The fly unerringly deposits its eggs in the warm receptacle, and the inexorable metamorphosis begins. Under ideal conditions, each egg begins within hours to move and assume the shape of a tiny worm. The "worm" grows steadily as it burrows into the tasty flesh and feeds for several days before dropping out of the wound to complete its development into a fly. Therefore an animal can sometimes keep the sore licked clean of additional "fly-blows" and after the "worms" drop out, the sore or wound heals itself. Much more often, especially during rainy years when flies are numerous, additional eggs are deposited daily, causing the wound to grow larger and larger.

Due to the success of an eradication program, screwworms

have not been a problem for twenty-five years or longer, though the threat still exists. But in the era under discussion they were the cowman's nemesis, and Gene spent most of each day trying to keep this menace in check. Added to this job was the ongoing maintenance of windmills and the corralling of my brother and me, who spent each summer at the ranch where we were too young to be of any help and too old to be restricted to the yard. It is plain to see that John was a little short-handed. Eventually, or much too soon—depending on the point of view—September arrived and school began, which probably made it easier for Daddy to find hands. At any rate, more cowboys were hired, and Gene was moved to town.

The Tascosa needed a bouncer, and Gene had all the qualifications, except imposing size. He was cool under pressure and had a persuasive manner; his lack of avoirdupois was not a real handicap, for word soon got around that it was risky business to put too much strain on his good nature. I got a good look at one of the fellows who probably helped spread the gospel. That misguided soul, driven by the fires of fervor and encumbered by a pathetic deficiency in judgment, pulled a knife. I saw Gene hit him and watched the knife arc to the floor about thirty feet away. As I picked it up and looked toward the door, Gene was coming back inside wearing a satisfied smile. He could be "kind of sudden" when his patience was stretched too thin.

As has been mentioned, the men who followed the booms were an independent lot. They were tough, opinionated individuals who grudgingly accepted instruction from even tougher bosses. For the most part, they were willing and able workmen who performed their tasks capably when on the job. But those stellar hands were quick to take offense, and even quicker to retaliate against any slur or intrusion while they were "relaxing" in town. Given this attitude and way of life, it naturally follows that the Tascosa had its fair quota of squabbles. There were fusses and fights and the rest of the problems that are inherent in that kind of business.

Yet the Kermit boom was somehow different—different from Wink and the earlier boomtowns of the twenties. There was the same rush by daring and imaginative men to secure leases and get that "black stuff" on top of the ground. There were the same boomtown followers, or at least the same type. There was the same boisterous exuberance and "devil take the hindmost" attitude. But something was missing.

Maybe it was the Volstead Act. That bane of mankind had been repealed, and the dispensers and consumers of liquor were no longer branded criminals. Booze was legal, each bottle was adorned with a tax stamp, and the Treasury was showing faint symptoms of health. The government might even have gone to the extreme of laying off some of the 'revenooers," but such a common sense move is unlikely, and no verification is at hand. Anyway, Kermit was positively overflowing with law-abiding citizens. Perhaps that was the "difference." The enormous cost of "habit regulation" should have been a lesson that would endure forever, but alas, it was not to be.

All the excitement in a honky-tonk is not spawned by belligerent men. John was trying to talk a woman who had indulged rather recklessly into modifying her language and keeping it at a suitable pitch. Believing these restrictions to be a blatant violation of her "right of free speech," she picked up a small stack of heavy metal trays, while John's attention was momentarily distracted, and brought them down with considerable force on top of his bald head. "Trays went all over the dance floor," John said with a grin. Gene was walking toward the front of the building when a tray sailed by his nose. He grabbed the obstreperous "lady" by her arms above each elbow, lifted her off the floor, and kept walking. "Aw,

I've been thrown out of better joints than this one," she bragged. "Maybe so," was the agreeable reply, "but not any quicker, I'll bet." John was still rubbing his aching head and wondering when his ears would stop ringing.

On another occasion, I was standing on a stool with an unobstructed view when Daddy was taken out of the action. A fight broke out on the dance floor, and John rushed back to help break up the "argument." When he tried to squeeze between two bystanders who were facing away from the fight, they stooped down; each man came up with a foot and shoved John headfirst under a table. John was helpless, and the two fellows held him in that position until someone else broke up the fight. The teamwork was impressive.

Just before I was chased back to the bedroom, someone asked Daddy: "Who were the guys that were fighting?"

"I don't know," he laughed, "I couldn't see much from under that table." John's capacity for spontaneous laughter at his own discomfiture was arguably his most endearing characteristic.

There was only one set-to, so far as I know, that could have been disastrous. Daddy said it was also the only time he ever saw Gene Forsythe lose his composure. On their way to the rig and facing the rigors of a morning tower, a driller and his crew dropped in for a "quick one." Daddy served the beer, and when he turned from the backbar with the driller's change, he was facing a cocked pistol in the hand of a man who had been ejected earlier in the evening.

The driller, who was standing next to the armed man, had a beer in one hand and was joking with his crew. He saw the pistol while reaching for his change and, with great presence of mind, slammed his free hand down on top of the gun just as the would-be assassin pulled the trigger. The gun failed to fire because the sharp solid firing pin that is part of the hammer stuck in that thin piece of flesh between the thumb and

forefinger of the driller's hand—and the fight for the gun was underway. The thug had a firm grip on the handle, and, if nothing else, he was strong and determined; the driller's crew jumped into the fray. Oil-treated pine awash in spilled beer is hazardous footing, and every man in the brawl was soon on the floor, maneuvering and straining for control of the pistol. Gene, who was some distance away, got a glimpse of the weapon, and knowing only that Daddy had been threatened, dove into that mass of flailing bodies and in very short order broke free of the melee with the gun in his hand.

"He seemed to be almost crazy mad," Daddy said. "He backed up a couple of steps and, using the pistol for emphasis, told those gentlemen in pretty strong language to stay where they were. I walked around to his side of the bar and, speaking as soothingly as I knew how, explained what had happened and asked for the gun. Gene looked down like he had forgotten what he was holding, shook his head a little, and handed it over. Then, still in a boiling rage, he jerked the gun-toter to his feet and threw him out again. That was the last time I ever saw the fellow." The driller was the only one who suffered an injury. At some time during the struggle, probably when Gene wrenched the gun from the hands of the grappling combatants, that thin piece of flesh which might have saved Daddy's life suffered an ugly, painful tear. It is not possible to properly express my regret that the driller's name cannot be recalled. I last heard it repeated about fifty years ago and should have carved it in stone at the time.

A lot of things happened while John was running the Tascosa—some of them funny and some aggravating. It was the nature of the business. One of the irritating incidents was when some disgruntled customer tossed a dynamite bomb under the front window. About fifty dollars took care of the damage but the noise was terrifying, at least to us kids. The place was closed and the family in bed, so the bomber wasn't trying to hurt anybody. Yet for some reason, John's fury reached epic proportions. He had a suspect and had he been sure, beyond a doubt, of the fellow's guilt, Daddy would have killed him. It is curious that such a little thing—by way of comparison—could so arouse his sense of outrage. He probably would not have been at all amused had he been present when I overheard some wag tell a waitress: "John must be in serious trouble with the local chapter of the W.C.T.U." But he wasn't there, and that bit of humor escaped me for several years.

The world was wonderful, at least from a child's outlook. Life in the back of a honky-tonk was filled with unique experiences. We had lined those two rooms in the back with cardboard from empty boxes in a fairly successful effort to stem the flow of cold north winds. Work was piling up at the ranch. Mama was getting ready to open a cafe. My brother and I got whipped by a little neighborhood killjoy and took our frustrations out on other kids—kids we could handle. What more could boys expect from life? But this enlightening exposure to the primitive impulses of man was not destined to continue.

Business was pretty good for two years; then there was a strike by the rig-builders' union which virtually shut down the oil field. John leased out the Tascosa, and the name was changed, but the strike went on, and at the end of a year the new operator gave it up. Daddy never reopened it; he dismantled about half the building and moved the other half to the ranch, where it is still being used for a barn. Exploration for oil in the county did not come to a standstill, but it never regained its former pace. That is the inevitable finale for every boom, but Kermit's period of prosperity was seriously restricted by a union which no longer exists. It died under the weight of jackknife rigs. John sent no condolences.

Gene Forsythe worked for John only three or four years, but they became friends for life. He is buried next to Daddy in a private grave site on the ranch they both loved, and I have to believe that Daddy is resting more comfortably with Gene once more at his side.

IX

Mama continued to operate her cafe for some time after Daddy converted his honky-tonk into a barn, but by the summer of 1939 the family was once more intact at the ranch. Gene and I were farmed out, for the last time, during the 1939-1940 school year. The 1940-1941 term saw us driving an old Model-A Ford to school, so Daddy must have concluded that we could do enough work to justify the additional expense. The following summer, at Mama Haley's insistence, the ranch started paying me the enormously satisfying sum of $25 a month. (Top hands were getting $60.) Because he was two years younger, Gene had to settle for $15. This wasn't called discrimination then. A worker's salary was based on his capability and production. The amount of our wages was Daddy's way of telling us that we were coming along, but had not "arrived." (He also had more direct methods of making his point.)

John's situation had changed somewhat, because the man who always made the final decisions, in business at least, was gone. Papa Haley died in December 1937, and each of his five children received a designated portion of the ranch surface. The minerals were passed on undivided—a fifth to each heir.

Mama Haley assumed Papa's interest in the cattle operation, and the name was changed to Mrs. J.A. Haley & Sons. A few years later the three girls sold their respective interests in the surface to Daddy and Evetts, who later made yet another division between themselves.

My recollections seem to jump from summer to summer. By that time of year in 1940, the war in Europe had been raging for months. From the outset John feared that our country would be drawn into the conflict, so he followed its progress with much interest and some trepidation. Foreseeing the shortages ahead, and with the blessings of Mama Haley and Evetts who shared his belief, he pushed hard to get the ranch ready for such an eventuality.

John used the limited funds available to buy a new pickup and stockpile critical materials and replacement parts. New windmills were perhaps the most important purchase of all. The windmill replacement project had already begun in a limited way, but the threat of war gave needed impetus. The old mills, with the direct stroke and wooden wheels, were finally giving way to more sophisticated mills which were geared and made entirely of steel. The geared mills turn in much softer wind and function with a minimum of maintenance. The Aermotor Company in Chicago made the most popular brand.

"Aermotor, the cowboy's friend" was the reverent accolade bestowed by Big John Loter, a grizzled and "stove-up" puncher. How right he was, but further explanation might be in order. This dry West Texas climate caused the thin wooden feathers (wind sails) in the old mills to shrink and fall out of the wheel. It was not unusual to see windmills turning with a third of their feathers missing, and all too often a strong sandstorm would scatter the entire wheel over an area the size of ten city blocks. About the only way to keep the feathers where they belonged, and out of the kindling pile, was to

wrap rawhide around each feather and the two thicker cross-braces to which they were attached—a chore nobody liked.

An old dry cowhide would be thrown in a water tank and soaked until it was soft and pliable. If other work intervened and the cowhide stayed in the water too long, it stunk. Boy did it stink! No matter, it was used anyway, which provided a strong incentive to be more prompt in the future. A cowboy, or maybe two, cut the hide into strips of an inch or so in width and with colorful, heartfelt profanity carried them to the top of the tower and "tied in" the feathers. Boys who were raised on a ranch in that era learned the necessary language long before they were up to the job.

That was only one irksome characteristic of those old mills. Another was that they were always shaking the braces loose from the tower legs. There must have been a hundred pounds of nails in some of the older towers. Yet another drawback was that every two or three days someone had to climb the tower and pour oil on the working parts.

Old crankcase oil was generally used, and the cowboy would take an uncomfortable seat astride the tail vane with his bottle or can of oil and "grease" the mill. In this position he always faced directly into the wind, and when the breeze was brisk he and his clothes acquired a mechanic's appearance. However, if the cowboy had been doctoring screwworms his vocation was never in doubt, for no mechanic ever smelled like that.

Once while engaged in such a chore, Daddy dropped a bottle of oil. It hit a girt and broke, an accident with no significance had Mama not been underneath. Her hair was soaked in oil and part of the broken bottle opened her scalp. The cut bled freely, and the mixture of coal black oil and blood turned her dark brown hair to an attractive shade of chestnut sorrel. She was not pleased. That is a bit of an understatement, but we had better abandon domestic mishaps and get back to comparing windmills.

The gears in the Aermotor turn in an oil bath which has to be changed but once a year. At least the factory strongly recommends this procedure. John complied, but a few old-timers balked. At the end of a year the oil in their mills didn't look a bit like the oil in their old pickups, and they considered this practice a disgraceful waste. Regardless of maintenance habits the Aermotor mill is durable, and it eliminated some bothersome chores. Melancholy yearnings for the "old days" never include Eclipse windmills.

John was forty-four years old on that Sunday morning when a masterful coup by the Japanese navy destroyed most of our warships at Pearl Harbor and all our arrogance. That so-called "sneak attack" (who notifies the enemy in advance?) was brilliantly executed, but it ignited a reaction in the American people for which the Japanese imperialists were not prepared. It awakened a slumbering rancor for Orientals in the hearts of millions and instantly instilled a steadfast determination to avenge the outrage. This implacable resolve rivaled the incredible bravery and fortitude of the Japanese fighting man, which our politicians and media cavalierly dismissed as "fanaticism." The "awakening" did not properly apply to John, for his warlike tendencies were never far from the surface, and they could be easily aroused without the stimulus of racial hostility.

He believed the rest of the family could somehow take care of the ranch and that his proper place was in the trenches. He was filled with a young man's desire and spirit, but two powerful forces blocked his way: Mama, and the ravages of asthma. He had asked for and received my mother's love, care and opinions in 1924. Asthma stormed in uninvited in 1926 and was to plague him the rest of his life. Combined, their opposition was too strong, and Daddy observed the war from the ranch—short handed, worked down, often laboring for breath and railing at fate.

Long before Pearl Harbor, Daddy put up a seven-volt windcharger, took the radio out of Mama's car and installed it in the house. Throughout the war, through the commentaries of Walter Winchell and others, he vicariously experienced every humiliating defeat and hard-won victory. No wonder he was exhausted before VJ Day. Yet John did not give in to frustration. There was too much to do.

In the summer of 1942, he sent Gene to Evetts' place in the Panhandle, left all the riding for me, and with a crew of three to five men put in a new watering, complete with corrals. He also drilled another well at an existing watering and put up a new mill. Though screwworms had nearly eaten us alive the year before, they were not too bad in 1942, and I was able to keep them under control. Daddy stayed with the rest of his crew, and, to use his favorite expression, "business sure picked up for awhile."

John built towers for the new mills out of angle iron and steel sucker rods. He was unfamiliar with such handy tools as cutting torches, drill presses, metal saws, et cetera, and never gave them a thought. He laid in plenty of coal, cleaned up the old manual forge, set the anvil in place, drug out the cold set, punches and sledgehammers, and went to work. Daddy and Jack Jackson, another small man about his age, did the measuring and marking and took turns cranking the forge, while two more powerful men spelled each other on the hammers. They built the towers in a surprisingly short time, and considering the tools, did so with amazing precision. It was hot, hard work in the middle of a sweltering summer. Clothes sweated out, and salt consumption jumped off the charts.

Daddy and his crew finished those projects in August, and two of the men went straight to the army. John was not apprehensive as he handed over their checks and said good-bye; he was envious. Excessively so, because he was just a year or so older than one of the hands. Adventure was overseas, and

86

being stuck in place was hard to accept.

Jack Jackson had been at the ranch all summer, and when the extra men left, Jack stayed on. In the process of growing up, Gene and I had been exposed to some fine cowboys, normal drinkers, and pretty good teachers—Lonnie Henderson and Joe Lamb to name just two. But Jackson was something different.

He was a butcher by profession, though he had done a little of everything. Jack was no cowboy, but he was the only non-cowboy I ever saw who never got in the way. At any other job on a ranch, he was the best you could find. He was not physically strong, but he had endurance. With bacon and a couple of biscuits each day and three hours sleep each night, Jack could work forever. He was Daddy's kind of hand.

Like most men of character, Jack nursed a number of pretty strong prejudices; moreover, they enjoyed plenty of exercise. Though he had worked for wages since his early teens, he held all labor unions in utter contempt. During the war John L. Lewis and his United Mine Workers threatened a strike and informed the world that strong picket lines would be posted. Daddy and Jackson were incensed. They were ranting and raving about this proposed disruption of the war effort when someone else at the breakfast table interposed a mild objection. "Well," began Jack's instant retort, "here's the way I look at it. If John is working me too hard, not paying enough and I decide to quit—that is my business, and he has no legitimate complaint. But if I stand in front of his gate with a pick-handle and keep everyone else from working, then that comes under the head of his business, and he has every right to use any means at hand to move me out of the way. Hell, if those union idiots knew how to run a business, they wouldn't be labor. They would own the company." That more or less concluded the discussion.

John L. Lewis campaigned vigorously against Roosevelt in

the President's successful bid for a third term. There was a lot of antipathy. Daddy and Jackson despised both men. They shared a firm and unshakable belief that no nation should be obliged to suffer a simultaneous onslaught by two such demagogues and spent many fruitless hours bemoaning the whimsy of fate. John was strictly business and Jack an incorrigible drunk; withal they were ideological twins.

Jack worked as a butcher or at any job he could find in the oilfield until the booze had him twenty pounds overweight, bloated and shaky. He would then seek work at the ranch, and Daddy always put him on. Jack never stayed over a few months at a time. When he was dried out to his own satisfaction he would quit and go back to town. And so it was that fall.

John went into the winter without any help, but the range was in pretty good shape and the cattle doing just fine. His running fight with asthma, however, was not going so well. Sometimes he would go for weeks without lying down. He slept in a chair or propped up in bed. It was the only way he could breathe. He didn't sleep much because he was up at all hours, wheezing, coughing, and banging a coffee pot down on the stove. He could make more noise in the kitchen than anyone living. How Mama and Gene got any rest was a mystery. Even the bunkhouse was too close for comfort, so I spent another winter in the barn.

X

John's forebodings had come to pass: the war effort was taking a toll. Tires, sugar and gasoline were rationed, and anything made of steel could not be found or was in short supply. Except for military use, cars and pickups were no longer manufactured. These are only a few of the items that were difficult or impossible to come by. If you were so ill-advised as to wonder aloud why lug wrenches were no longer in stock, the merchant looked at you condescendingly and growled, "There is a war on. Haven't you heard?" (The same response was heard in every army and navy supply depot overseas. The only difference was those fellows threw in several additional comments about your inability to grasp a situation.)

Daddy was philosophical about material shortages, for he had planned well and was a recognized expert at makeshift. It was the unavailability of hands that worried him. He needed help for the day-to-day operation of the ranch. When a full crew was needed for working cattle, he could and did lean heavily on the neighbors. Since ranches have been under fence, most owners have considered it an act of courtesy to advise a neighbor when they plan to work any country adjoining his pasture or pastures. The rancher with the common boundary, after being so advised, either sends someone or comes himself. When the work is over, all stray cattle picked up in the drives will be taken back home. During and immediately after World War II, the practice of neighboring filled a vital need.

A few ranchers, for one reason or another, did not like to swap work, but John and Tom Linebery exploited the practice to such a degree that they almost ran the two outfits as one. They pooled their resources to work cattle, fix windmills and in extreme circumstances, patch corrals. I once heard a cowboy jokingly tell a waitress that he really didn't know who he worked for. Still, because of the general shortage of hands, some things, such as mending fences, just didn't get done, and many ranches during this period fell into a mild state of disrepair.

John managed the spring work in 1943 with the help of old men, kids and neighbors. After the branding and "shaping up" Gene and I were his only hands. That was of little concern, for Daddy had things pretty well in hand. A fairly new horse trailer, strategic crossfencing, plus new waterings and new windmills at old waterings enabled the three of us to answer every need of the livestock. We were plenty busy, but every evening Daddy dutifully sat down by the radio for his daily dose of discouraging world news. At that time, however, his primary source of concern was Mama Haley.

She was being treated for cancer of the throat, and the results were not encouraging. Daddy was worried. Everybody, with the possible exception of Mama Haley, was worried. During her irregular visits to the ranch she was cheerful and uncomplaining, never allowing anyone to dwell on her illness, at least in her presence. Nevertheless, even the Mama Haleys of this world must yield to the inevitable. She died in October 1943 and left a vacuum that has never been filled.

Her interest in the cattle was willed to Daddy and Evetts,

and three or four years later they elected to divide the cattle as well as the ranch. When a date was set for the work to begin, the neighbors were notified, and as usual Tom Linebery was there. We penned Evetts' portion of the cattle just before noon, and after a hasty meal, proceeded to brand them. The big calves were stripped from their mammies and branded first. They had been worked in the spring and needed nothing but Evetts' brand, so we put them through the "squeeze." The sun was merciless, as it usually is, and for a radius of twenty feet the big branding fire added several degrees. The work was well organized. Daddy was leading off, and he had men horseback loading the crowding pens, Tom Linebery and I working the squeeze chute, and the rest of the crew prodding the bawling calves down the branding chute to the "squeeze." Evetts was branding, and he couldn't keep up. Tom and I had the only job that permitted any extended conversation, and he was giving his ever-present wit full rein—one of Tom's more admirable traits when the hours drag on in dust-filled corrals.

Evetts rushed back and forth in a trot which quickly eased to a shuffling walk. In less than an hour, sweat filled his eyes, and his dirt-caked face resembled a river delta as perspiration poured through tiny waterways to the end of his nose and chin. Tom was still laughing and telling stories. Apparently the levity was grating on Evetts' nerves. "You fellows are sure having a hell of a lot of fun," he grumbled. Tom, without missing a chuckle, replied, "Evetts, I learned a long time ago that when you come over to help Mr. John, if you don't have fun when you're working, you're just plumb out of luck for fun." Evetts conceded the validity of this observation but somehow gave the impression that unrestrained hilarity under such conditions might indicate a warped personality. Tom was unabashed. The hint of a stagger in Evetts' familiar gait drew Daddy's attention, and he took over the branding job. Then

Tom started ragging him for not spelling his brother sooner. "Let me tell you, John," he shouted across the chute, "when you let a man get in Evetts' shape before he gets some relief, it slows down the work, and I have to get home in time to milk." Evetts had cooled off a bit, and the color of his face was approaching normal, so he found Tom's nagging remarks a little more humorous. Daddy just laughed, and except when branding or switching irons, never slowed from a trot.

This particular work took place after the war, and it is illustrative of all the operations for several years. John cooperated with every adjoining rancher, but for so long as Daddy lived, Linebery performed above and beyond the call of a good neighbor.

The one thing John had not anticipated was that even after the war the availability of ranch hands would never get back to what he considered normal. Gone were the days when he could drive over to Pecos and find at least one pretty good hand who had just spent his last dime in a local bar. That doesn't mean he always came back from town empty-handed. All too often he brought a "hand" to the ranch who had been rejected by every rancher from five adjacent counties. That was often worse than having nobody at all, and John's prickly temper was much in evidence until he let the fellow go.

"That just kills my soul" was an oft-used expression that filled careless cowboys with dread. The lament usually split the air as John viewed the dismal results of unforgivable negligence, and the guilty puncher knew that additional comments would be forthcoming. Throughout the forties the incompetence of most available hands plus two teen-aged boys occasioned quite a bit of wear and tear on John's "soul." The cow herd, however, never suffered from inattention. Barns and fences might display signs of neglect, but the cattle never wanted for anything that man could provide.

From a monetary point of view, Daddy was not a great cowman. In the realm of caretaking or the handling of livestock, he was one of the best—a marvelous cowboy who could handle any job on a ranch. John was a pretty good mechanic and carpenter, a fair blacksmith, and he could fix anything about a windmill. He could drill a water well and dress his own tools; he could build forms and pour concrete. He did all those things and more, but there was a drawback. Daddy never could see any reason why his kids could not be as proficient. Though Gene came close to matching those skills, I did not. I have no mechanical talent whatever, am virtually helpless with hammer and saw, and never did take to drilling rigs. Daddy persevered.

He was a natural-born teacher and knew from experience that his lessons, if heeded, would eliminate a lot of grief. This fact was lodged in Daddy's consciousness because Papa Haley was a businessman. He bought and sold ranches and herds of cattle, along with other endeavors, but his interest was economic and the actual handling of livestock held little appeal. Therefore Daddy acquired his skills by doing, and he paid the price for every mistake. Nevertheless, he was an apt student, and by the time Gene and I arrived on the scene he had become a master of that fine art. It was a long while before either of us realized the extent of such an advantage. Through the years there have been a lot of good cowboys who never let their kids learn. The youngsters received plenty of verbal instruction, but somehow they were denied the opportunity of practical experience. That was not Daddy's way: what is now known as "on the job training" suited him better. From our early teens he had us doing everything from tying off a mill in order to splice a broken cutoff wire to delivering a calf from flat on our bellies in the icy mud. We did the hundreds of things that must be done on a ranch over and over until they became routine.

Most important of all, through genetics and training, he passed on his gift for handling horses and cattle. After the necessary instructions, he turned us loose with livestock to determine if any of the lessons had soaked in. From the time we could more or less handle a horse, he constantly admonished: "Keep your eyes on the cattle. Pay attention," he would yell. "If you watch the cattle, you can avoid a lot of wrecks by turning them back before they work up any steam." Signs of comprehension must have been rare, as throughout our formative years he stressed again and again the value of alertness and anticipation. We were taught how to read warning signals and what precautions to take, when to crowd up and when to give slack, and what seemed like a thousand other tests of our judgment.

As each of us reached the age of thirteen, we started learning the joys and frustrations of working alone. Daddy mounted us on good horses and sent us our respective ways to doctor worms and tend to anything else that needed attention. We did not always prowl for worms alone, but it was the beginning of that critical phase of learning. To be a good hand a boy must eventually learn — and the sooner the better — to do everything that must be done with livestock, while relying solely on himself and his horse. After a couple of years apprenticeship, Daddy sent us out on broncs to do the same job. Forthwith, a lot more cattle were doctored in the chute. A snaky bronc inspires second thoughts about reaching for a rope. Being deprived of an older hand's counsel and the services of a dependable cowhorse puts an awful strain on a kid. He has to think for himself. If he is up to this task, his long-suffering sire might own up to parentage.

There were times, however, when Daddy's demonstrations were at odds with his instructions. In our mid-teens, Gene and I were just beginning to experience the rapture induced by fast horses and manila ropes. Our exuberance got us in trouble, and we were thoroughly dressed down for being too rough on cattle, especially the cows. "Don't be fairgrounding my cows," Daddy stormed, "or you're gonna cripple something. When you have to doctor a cow outside, do it like I showed you. Bring her to a stop, wrap her up and pull her down."

This method probably lessens the odds of crippling a cow, but riding around an active thousand-pound animal until your rope chances upon a proper hitch can be difficult and is always time consuming. It makes a hand wish he could head and heel the big cattle, but alas, that requires a partner. We were usually too shorthanded to afford this luxury, so Gene and I vowed to keep much closer tabs on Daddy's whereabouts.

About a week later we were working a herd at the house. Part of the crew penned the cut and one contrary old cow came back by them at the gate. I was working between the herd and cut and helped a couple of cowboys hold her up as Daddy got down and cinched up. He took his rope down, joined the other two fellows and started her to the pens again. Daddy was well-mounted, but the cow hooked his horse out of her way and headed for the roundup. She did not get far before John's loop settled neatly around both horns, and he threw a trip which offered solid proof that he had not always been so concerned about pampering his cattle. That dun horse really "bedded her down," and the cow had barely regained her feet before he was driving by her again. When the cow went down that time, Daddy jumped from his horse and filled her eyes full of dirt. When he felt her vision was sufficiently improved, he jerked the rope off, and that old "bunch quitter" almost ran over the cowboy who was minding the gate as she sought the safety of corrals in a dead run. It appeared that cantankerous bovine had some small capacity for reason, and had Gene and I known how to communicate, we could have told her that defying John Haley was pushing imprudence to the brink of fatuity.

I personally feel most indebted to Daddy for what he taught us about handling horses. When a cowboy is breaking broncs, he encounters runaway horses, pawing horses, kicking horses, pitching horses and an occasional individual that has all those characteristics. Daddy was a small man, and we were undersized kids, so we learned to take every advantage. He worked with us for a while in the bronc pen, helping us out and giving constant advice. His advice and demonstrations were invaluable, but there comes a time when a boy must be left to his own devices. He cannot learn to judge the temperament of a horse, the power, the incredible quickness or the deceptive range of those slashing feet except through personal experience. Daddy easily recognized the time of transition. He stood aside and shouted encouragement or surrendered to helpless laughter as we took our educational lumps. In the following years he came forth with suggestions only when the need was obvious

XI

August 1944 to June 1946 found me engaged with some rather important assignments. My instruments were brooms, swabs, scrub brushes, paring knives and undersized shovels. (The last were used primarily for latrine excavations.) Due no doubt to my skill with these tools, Japan was inexorably forced to her knees. In the meantime, according to Mama's letters, Daddy was having a rough time with asthma. His condition must have improved dramatically, for following my return to the ranch there was no visible difference in his man-killing pace.

"We've got to catch up," he explained. "We've been losing ground for several years." That probably sounded reasonable to newcomers, but those of us who knew him never cherished any dreams about catching up. Daddy loved to work, and overdrive was his only gear. Fortunately, additional help arrived in January 1947 in the person of a young cowboy named Chalmer Davis. He was a workhorse, and while he was on the job "things got done."

The moisture was skimpy in 1946, and John sold half the cattle that fall. We still had 400 cows and were blissfully unaware of the dry years ahead. By 1950 we concluded that

Demeter, the goddess of agriculture long revered by farmers of yore, must have taken time off for the most prolonged bender in the history of Olympus. Rainfall did not cease abruptly, but the country was easing into the longest drouth that any old-timer could call to mind. As a result, life on the ranch was sometimes hectic and always unsettled. Chal worked there at least two different times, and both Gene and I were in and out. Sometimes Daddy had the three of us, sometimes two, and occasionally only one. From time to time, even less steady cowboys answered the call. The drouth was not solely responsible for the constant rotation of hands. Sooner or later, with the possible exception of Chalmer, fatigue forced every cowboy to ask for his time. He had to work somewhere else for a while in order to rest.

Few men are blessed with Chal's endurance. Physical exhaustion, however, was not the principal reason for the periodic departure of dedicated hands. The strange truth is this: when a hand worked for Daddy for any extended period, his nervous system played out first. Somehow, a constant and pervasive sense of urgency emanated from Daddy's presence, like unending breakers spawned by the restless sea. The situation was and is somewhat mystifying, for he never said or did anything, at least nothing discernible, that would cause such a feeling. Every now and then something in the nature of a crisis arose, and it always found John at his best. Usually the problem was so quickly, skillfully and matter-of-factly disposed of that no mental torment had time to take hold. There was no enervation from real crises; on the contrary, they tended to stimulate. How anybody, especially unknowingly, could make routine maintenance assume the aspect of life or death is likely a question that will never be answered.

Daddy had not the remotest idea that such a circumstance existed. If he was ever puzzled about why strong young men half his age could not keep up, it was never voiced. And, had anyone been brash enough to propound the predicament, John would have regarded him with sympathy—and recommended a dose of calomel. (In my childhood, calomel was the panacea for all undiagnosed ailments.) Nevertheless, the situation did exist, and it eventually sapped the vitality and will from every hired hand. Conversely, Daddy was happy and content. "We're gettin' things done around here." That was the status quo for years. Cowboys came and went, and in between asthma attacks, Daddy maintained the same grueling pace, whether working alone or with a crew—until arteriosclerosis took a hand.

Immediately following the diagnosis, John's activities were not greatly impaired. For varying lengths of time, he was much as always, but the relentless restriction of blood flow was exacting a fee. The periods of activity became farther apart and of shorter duration, and that dynamic force gradually subsided to an occasional sputter. The drouth ended in 1958, and from that time his condition steadily deteriorated.

Daddy and Mama had been living in Kermit since 1956, and my brother was at the ranch. John never gave in to his disability and believed with no reservation that without his daily presence not one thing would ever be properly done. As so often happens when an active man becomes infirm, he wasted so much of Gene's time discussing the jobs that a lot of them did not get done. To invoke a cliché, Gene's patience was sorely tried. Worse yet, Daddy himself might have been aware of the situation and powerless to make an adjustment. The aging process is brutal.

During one of his daily visits, he elected to help Gene doctor a cow. In the process of tying her down, Daddy broke an ankle and started hobbling toward the barn. "If you'll wait a minute," Gene urged, as he was "wrapping up" the cow's two bottom feet, "I'll take you to the barn in a wheelbarrow and go get the pickup."

"Hell no, you'd probably turn the damn thing over and break my other leg." Having made that irrational decision, Daddy set out immediately on what must have seemed like a marathon, though it was only about fifty yards.

Besides rushing headlong into situations he could no longer handle, John adopted the habit of wandering all over the ranch in his car. Seldom did anyone know his whereabouts because his aimless meandering was completely devoid of reason or routine. The trunk of his car always contained a cardboard box packed with coffee pot, coffee, bread and bacon, and sometimes half the tools on the ranch. That miniature chuck box was a welcome sight when Daddy once invited me to get down and join him for dinner. "Trim up a couple of green mesquite limbs. By the time coffee is ready the fire will be burned down and we can broil some bacon." Since it was way past noon and still seven miles to the house, I was only too happy to help Daddy eat up the last of his bacon.

Gene told me Daddy also had a compulsion to climb to the top of every windmill. That was no easy task for a man who could not walk from his car to the front door without resting. About halfway up the ladder he would stop to recover his wind and, more often than not, take a couple of nitroglycerin tablets, then slowly make his way to the platform. This habit was worrisome, if nothing more, for we half expected that someday he would be found beyond help at the foot of a windmill tower.

Gene was paying for his raising, because Daddy was also prone to saddle up when no one was around and take off by himself on a horse he had no business riding. Only twice, to my knowledge, did this result in an injury. Once, while he was trying to mount, a horse spun away from him and broke John's ankle. He was seventy years old, and his scarred, oft-used crutches were relatively dust-free when the second and last mishap occurred.

101

Gene found him about a quarter of a mile southeast of the house after his horse came into the corrals with an empty saddle. Daddy was unable to stand and subsequently the x-rays showed that a "loop" on the bottom of the pelvis had been broken on both sides, leaving a half-inch gap on one side, nearly twice that much on the other. I was living in Midland at the time, and within twenty-four hours after the horse threw him, Daddy was on the phone. He was unhappy, if such an understatement is permissible.

"Old Mac [Dr. McClure] tells me that he won't operate and tie those damn bones back together," he roared as I held the phone as far from the ear as my hand could reach. "He says if we keep the bed cranked up near a sitting position that in a few days the gap might close a little, but he refuses to operate in any case. By God they're my bones, and I want 'em tied back together."

I finally got Daddy somewhat pacified by arguing that it would be prudent to be as patient as possible until he learned the degree of closure. I also suggested that he ask for an opinion from Dr. Saddler, an excellent orthopedist who practiced in Amarillo.

Dr. McClure was more than happy to comply with this request, and my phone rested peacefully in its cradle for a few days. Then, "Saddler says he won't operate," Daddy yelled in my ear before I realized my aural health was at risk. "By God I want something done about this." He could complain to me only by telephone, and I was reasonably certain that Gene would always be too busy to answer his phone. That left Mama as the designated appeaser, and I shuddered in sympathy.

The upshot was that I called Dr. Saddler at home that night.

"How is your daddy?" he asked when I identified myself.

"Well, he was doing pretty good until he got your report," I replied.

"I thought that was a good report," Saddler said. "Have you seen it?"

"No sir."

"All right John. First of all, no reputable doctor is going to operate on your Daddy at his age, and in his condition, for that kind of break. His doctor sent me two sets of x-rays, and the last ones taken indicate that the gaps have narrowed about fifty percent. Now then, the bones will not knit together, but they will form a fibrous union. There is no structural stress in that area, and after the trauma of the break has passed and the union completed, he can do anything he wants, with no discomfort. Until then? As far as I am concerned, he can start moving around a little right now, if he can stand the pain." In essence, Dr. Mac had already told his patient the very same thing.

I drove to Kermit, carefully explained all this to Daddy, and firmly insisted that he give up the idea of pinning those bones. He listened without comment, and at last, seemed to accept the doctors' prognosis. I should have known better.

A few weeks later he packed his bag and told Mama he was going to spend a few days in Fort Worth. It was months before we learned that he drove straight to Temple, checked himself into Scott and White Clinic, and demanded that they patch him up properly. Following x-rays and the other necessary tests, the Scott and White doctor reported with a smile: "Mr. Haley, we should write you up. Through the years, asthma has taken over half your lung capacity, you are diabetic and have a rather serious heart condition. I am happy to say that in regard to the break, you can do anything the rest of your body can stand. The pelvis has healed completely, and there is nothing we or anybody else can do to make it better." Daddy was furious. The break never bothered him at all in the few short years that were left, but he never forgave any doctor involved for "making such a mess of patching me up." And no, the injury did nothing to dampen his enthusiasm for perching thirty feet above the ground to watch his cattle come in to water.

A long story but indicative of John's pertinacity. The saddest consequence of those clogged arteries was the mental deterioration. Daddy had always been a careful and deliberate thinker; he was never stampeded into anything. That characteristic can be comforting to a family. Fast talkers selling "deals" wasted little time on such an unresponsive prospect. He listened to their spiels, but never once made an impulsive decision. Now it had become virtually impossible for him to make a decision at all. Shaping up a herd became a prolonged and wearying chore. John debated with himself, and sometimes with others—often at length—the advisability of every cull. Even so, he often went to the cut and brought a cow back. He simply could not make up his mind.

Daddy had always engaged in physical pursuits; he did not know how to idle. He read almost nothing but depressing political reports, and, other than governmental affairs, his only interest was the ranch. He was plagued with frustration. Doubly so, because John was a strong adherent of the outdated philosophy that living is something more than just staying alive.

It should be explained right now that we are not talking about indulging an appetite. Daddy was never much of a drinker. He never knew that the proper intake of alcohol will make a man feel big, tough, rich and amorous. On the other hand, he never suffered the agony of thundering hoofbeats locked in rhythm with his throbbing head. He never smoked in his life, but more than likely Daddy rejected that habit due to the expense, waste of time, and later on, of course, the incompatibility of tobacco and asthma. He was a good eater and enjoyed good food, but the main reason he took time off for meals was the need for fuel. This is a roundabout way of saying that John was certainly no hedonist. He did not believe in humoring himself; that sort of thing was restricted to special holidays. He believed in goals, and his conviction that every man has a purpose and an inherent duty to strive for that end was unshakable. Had he ever taken the trouble to look up the meaning of nihilism, he would have been appalled. Webster's first definition is: "A viewpoint that traditional values and beliefs are unfounded and that existence is senseless and useless." I am quite certain Daddy never knew people with such ideas existed, or he would have suggested shooting the idiots and putting them out of their misery. As Eugene Manlove Rhodes might have said: "John was impatient, intolerant and prejudiced, but there was a streak of kindness in him."

Such attitudes or beliefs were not John's concept of living. In his lexicon, life or living meant experience, the by-product of adventure (or maybe it is the other way around), and steadfast adherence to a course that would provide for himself and his family. Security, in its usual sense, was to be disdained; the word itself ruffled his feathers. Security, especially unearned security, is the bane of mankind. It kills the desire to excel and eventually subdues the will, whereas, uncertainty is a necessary ingredient in the recipe for zestful living. It eliminates complacency, and compels a man to do his best. Security, as a welfare prop, cheapens life, impoverishes taxpayers, and has virtually destroyed the nation's fiber. That was the core of John's argument. An attempt to explore the subject in depth in his terminology would propel the price of pulpwood plumb but of sight, and his probable diatribe on today's conditions overwhelms the imagination.

Like every individual who does his own thinking, John was something of a paradox. A determined and relentless fighter who neither asked nor gave any quarter, he was the definition of tenderness when nursing sick animals or children. A man given to violence, he once sat at a sister's bedside and wept because she could not control a drinking problem. Daddy was never petty or mean, and a forgiving nature often got in the way of his resolve to be hard and unyielding. One reliable constant was his keen perception of the ridiculous. Eccentricities and bizarre incidents were not the only things that sent him into paroxysms of contagious laughter, but whatever the cause, those moments of merriment never escaped his selective memory, and he loved to share them with convivial companions.

A series of strokes rendered Daddy bedfast for over seventeen months before that great heart was mercifully stilled by pneumonia. Hovering ever within reach, his faithful sense of humor never deserted him. He died about ten o'clock in the evening, February 16, 1972.

The family and a host of friends were present when John was buried at the ranch. Predictably—since John had joined the church a few years previously—the preacher assured us that Daddy's soul was in Heaven, enshrouded by "eternal peace." Such declarations are a preacher's job, and his smug assurances are usually welcomed by grieving survivors. I sincerely believe, however, that if John Haley's new "homestead" does not include conflict, drouths, blizzards, sandstorms, towering rain clouds with awesome displays of lightning, and the sounds of thunder, from its distant rumble to its nearby earsplitting crack, if he cannot have friends, foes, a note at the bank, fat cattle, a mount of good horses, and see grama grass headed out, then all that "peace" is not going to project a heavenly aspect. Unless? Unless somehow Heaven can reprogram a cowboy's soul to be content with less than his normal fare in The Great Southwest.

DATE DUE
